The Bosses

The Bosses

Edited by

John D. Haeger
Central Michigan University

Michael P. Weber
Carnegie-Mellon University

Revised Edition

FORUM PRESS

Cover Photo: © June 1969,
American Heritage Publishing Company, Inc.

Contents

Preface

For more than a century political bosses have dominated the governments of American cities. Boss Tweed of New York, Curley of Boston, and Pendergast of Kansas City, all controlled and influenced the lives of citizens within their respective cities. Although the most famous and colorful bosses controlled large industrial centers, smaller cities throughout the nation also experienced boss rule. Each boss stamped his own personality on the city. Political bosses, however, shared certain common characteristics. By examining boss rule in several periods and in different cities one begins to discern its similar and unique features.

The book is divided into two parts. Part 1 examines bossism in New York from Boss Tweed to the turn of the century. The introductory essay provides a brief review of the historical forces which brought about machine politics and a basic description of the political machine's operation. Each reading then highlights a particular aspect of bossism through both primary and secondary sources. This part includes a portrait of Boss Tweed by a contemporary, a description of the relationship between bosses and immigrants, a humorous yet truthful account of a ward captain, an analysis of the emerging industrial corporation's ties to the political machine, plus a defense of the system by Richard Croker.

Part 2 is concerned with the twentieth century boss. The introductory essay outlines the basic changes in the physical size, population, and governmental structure of American cities since 1900. Each succeeding essay analyzes the changes in the boss system at various periods in the twentieth century. Frederick C. Howe first relates his experiences while working for Cleveland's reform mayor, Thomas L. Johnson, at the turn of the century. Lyle Dorsett next describes the Pendergast's control of Kansas City during the depression when the federal government made its first intrusion into the government of American cities. The following two essays, by author David Halberstam and Chicago newspaperman, Mike Royko, examine every facet of Richard J. Daley's recent political machine in Chicago. In the final essay, two political scientists question whether bossism as a political system can continue to exist in our sophisticated, technological society.

John D. Haeger
Michael P. Weber

The Nineteenth·Century Political Boss

The Development of Bossism

SINCE THE MID-NINETEENTH CENTURY, the political boss
has been a familiar figure in city government. Because of the
frequency of this form of municipal leadership, stereotypes of
the boss abound throughout American literature. According to
the image, the boss was short, stout, and from an immigrant
background. More often than not, he was a good-hearted
Irishman whose only real vices were a propensity toward cigars
and smoke-filled rooms. Invariably each boss served his
political apprenticeship in a local political organization rising
to power by strict adherence to the party's rules. While his
critics may have stressed his lack of education and social
graces, no one questioned his attention to hard work,
friendship, and loyalty. The boss was also a man of the people.
The duties of city office were never so onerous as to prevent
him from attending ethnic celebrations, drinking at local bars,
or mourning the death of a friend at a neighborhood wake.
Such practices made the boss a lovable rogue, but a rogue
nonetheless. Americans generally believed that bossism was
synonymous with corruption, that it violated the normal codes
of political service requiring honesty and efficiency, and that it

did not represent a government of skilled and dedicated public servants.

In recent years, scholars have challenged the stereotype etched in the popular imagination. Not all bosses originated from immigrant or lower class backgrounds, nor did they depend solely on immigrant populations for political support. Many bosses were educated, articulate, and capable administrators. While vague images led scholars to label bossism as ineffective and immoral, intensive study forced experts to credit bosses with reforms of city governments, progressive social attitudes toward minority groups, and effective administrations. Scholars thus saw bossism as a complex phenomenon which had little relationship to the popular stereotype.

How then does one identify a boss? He operated within a political machine, basically a political organization in the business of obtaining votes in order to stay in office. The organization views city hall in terms of jobs and economic influence while ideological issues are of secondary importance. This personal interest necessitates that machines be carefully organized and controlled. A machine worker, the ward leader, supervises each political division of the city. The ward leader makes the machine relevant to the citizens of his ward by fixing tickets at city hall, delivering baskets of food to needy families, or simply listening to the troubles of residents in their day-to-day efforts to survive. The boss welds the various elements of the organization together determining who gets what and keeping the different elements at peace. Whether through force of his personality or the use of political power, the boss must maintain rigid discipline to insure the machine's survival.

Bossism first appeared in the mid-nineteenth century as a response to the changing economic and social conditions of American cities. Industrial growth transformed cities from cohesive geographic and economic units into sprawling giants with diverse economic and racial groups. In the period from 1870 to 1900, nearly fourteen million immigrants arrived on American soil, the majority of whom located in urban areas.

During the same period, an even larger number of native Americans fled the unprofitable agricultural lands of New England to seek their fortunes in the burgeoning industrial metropolises. Between 1870 and 1900 New York City's population grew from slightly over a million to 3,500,000, creating almost insurmountable problems in housing, education, transportation, police, and fire protection. Technology responded with incredible speed to meet the challenge. From a horse-driven omnibus in 1850, for example, transportation improvements advanced from the steam-powered railroad to the elevated electric railway, to the subway system by 1904. But these improvements could never quite overtake the city's demands. When transportation facilities improved, new problems emerged in housing and sanitation as more people pressed into urban areas.

The chaos engendered by population growth and technological change was further complicated by inadequate city governments. Since the colonial period, municipal governments had developed in a haphazard fashion. Before the Civil War strong centralized governments were not required because most cities had only local business needs and fairly homogeneous populations. The physical dimensions of Boston and Philadelphia, for example, were small enough that an individual could walk from one end to the other in a day. When problems did arise, cities responded on an ad hoc basis or turned for aid to the state legislature from whom they derived their legal powers. As city problems multiplied in the mid-nineteenth century, city governments found that the legal tie to the state hindered effective action. State legislatures observed the city's rising crime statistics and the strange ethnic groups who refused to adopt the "American way" and labeled them as dens of moral iniquity. The persistent American ideal that cities were unhealthy and dangerous to democracy buttressed the state's viewpoint. State legislatures often refused to vote additional monies or to alter a city charter thereby preventing the city's response to new social problems. When state governments did act, they carefully maintained

control of the expanding city governments by establishing
separate agencies or boards for each new function such as
public education, sanitation, or transportation. Thus grafted
onto the existing city governments, states and sometimes the
cities themselves created a bewildering maze of independent
boards and agencies. Their functions and powers were never
carefully delineated. In New York City of the late 1860's, for
example, there were four agencies with the authority to tear
up the streets, but not one had the clear authority to repair
them. As constituted, city governments could not bring order.

The rise of the boss was also facilitated by a change in the
personnel available for municipal office. In the pre-1850
period, wealthy merchants and aristocrats who felt obliged to
devote some time to public service held city offices. Their task
was one dimensional since government's principal function was
to provide a suitable environment for local business. As city
governments were increasingly forced to mediate the varying
demands of industries and ethnic groups, the wealthy aristocrats declined further participation. The new economic leaders, who were developing fortunes in industry and commerce,
had little time for active public service. Their economic
horizons, moreover, had broadened. With developments in
transportation, businesses expanded their markets and influence beyond the city's boundaries thereby necessitating their
involvement in state and national politics.

Urban leadership positions were filled now by men who
possessed a different view of municipal office. The new city
leaders were professional politicians who saw public service as
a career. Similar to other careers in business of the late
nineteenth century, the professional city politician expected a
financial return on his investment of time.

Diversity, disorder, and change then characterized the city
from 1860 to 1900. Industrial growth changed the physical
structure of the city and spurred a technological revolution
which acted like a magnet drawing more people and businesses
into the city. Merchants, industrialists, and laborers each
demanded that the city respond to their needs. Immigrant

groups huddled in ethnic ghettos, lacking education, skills, and an acquaintance with American society, depended upon government to provide at least a token step toward the dream of success. But municipal governments merely reflected the chaos of the larger society. They were unprepared to cope with the myriad of problems induced by urbanization. The informal government of the merchant aristocrats plus the tangled legal relationships with states delayed prompt action. Who or what was to bring order?

The political party and its leader, the boss, was the one institution which cut across the varying economic, political, and social interests. Without a particular interest of his own other than power and personal aggrandizement, the boss centralized government and offered services to all the competing groups. Through the local ward organization, immigrants found their first identification with American society. When immigrants needed help in difficulties with the law, food to ease a jobless period, and even employment, ' ; ward leader was always there. In exchange, the immigrant gave his loyalty and vote to the boss. Businessmen supported the boss in order to obtain lucrative city contracts for street repair, a favorable court decision, or the regulation of a competing enterprise. In return, businessmen provided financial support either through direct grants or illegal kickbacks on city contracts. City government itself benefited because the boss utilized the political party to bring order to the various boards and agencies. When a street needed repair or a sanitary sewer had to be installed, the boss could move quickly through an otherwise confusing bureaucracy. The boss often extended his influence to the state level so that the city could garner additional tax monies or a more powerful city charter. While bossism did not function on a high ideological level, it did provide the government which cities lacked.

The Tweed Ring

William Marcy Tweed is ordinarily credited with being the first city boss. He rose to power in the late 1850's at precisely the moment that New York City's government was severely handicapped by the problems associated with a growing population and industrial concentration. Tweed and his colorful companions controlled New York City until 1871 when reformers revealed wholesale corruption in city hall.

The Tweed Ring has become the model for all later stereotypes of the boss. His audacity and greed in bilking New York City's municipal government often led observers to neglect a study of the background factors which brought Tweed to power. He did succeed in gaining several needed improvements for the city and provided the immigrants with a sense of belonging. The selection which follows, however, sees little positive good in Tweed's rule. Frank Goodnow's essay was first published in 1888 in James Brice's classic study of American politics, The American Commonwealth, *Bryce, an Englishman, analyzed every facet of American political and social life finding that America's one conspicuous failure was*

*the governing of cities. Goodnow's essay then was a bitter,
although not always accurate, attack on the Tweed Ring.*

The year 1857 marks an important epoch in the history of
the city of New York. It may be taken as the date of a great
change in the character of the population of the city — a
change which has vastly increased the difficulties of municipal
government, and presented problems whose solution has unfortunately not yet been attained. The middle classes, which
had thus far controlled the municipal government, were displaced by an ignorant proletariat, mostly of foreign birth,
which came under the sway of ambitious political leaders and
was made to subserve schemes of political corruption such as
had not before been concocted on American soil.

The year 1857 is also the date of a great change in the
legal position of the city. Down to this time all charters, and
almost all laws affecting the government of the city, were
either framed or suggested by the municipal authorities or
made to depend for their validity on the approval of the
people. But in 1857 the legislature committed itself finally and
definitely to the doctrine that it might change at will the city
institutions, framing the municpal government and distributing
the municipal powers as it saw fit. Since this date the largest
city of the American continent has lain at the mercy of the
state legislature; and the legislature has not scrupled to remodel and disarrange the governmental institutions of the city.
Its charter has been subjected to a continual "tinkering" that
has made the law uncertain and a comprehension of its administration extremely difficult. . . .

By the system of municipal government inaugurated in
1857 it will be noticed that the common council had very
little power. The most influential authorities were the mayor
and the executive boards and officers, in part elected by the
voters of the city, in part appointed by the central government

From James Bryce, *The American Commonwealth* (New York and
London: MacMillan & Co., 1888).

of New York State. This was the general character of the
government that New York possessed when it fell into the
hands of a band of "statesmen" of more than average ability
and of quite phenomenal dishonesty, whose career constitutes
the greatest reproach that has ever been cast upon popular
government.

The chief figure among the new rulers of the city was
William Marcy Tweed. Of Scotch parentage and a native of the
city, he started in life as a chairmaker, but growing weary of
the quiet ways of trade, found a position more to his liking in
one of the volunteer fire companies of the city, of which he
soon became foreman. Free and easy in his manners, loyal to
his friends, with great animal spirits and a large fund of coarse
humour, Tweed was just the man to be popular with the class
from which the fire companies were recruited; and his popularity among the "boys" of the fire brigade gave him an entrance
into "city politics." His first appearance in public life was
made in 1850, when he was elected an alderman of the city. In
this position he exhibited all the characteristics which afterwards made him famous. Any job or contract that would yield
him either pecuniary or political advantage found in him a
ready supporter; and so well did he make use of his opportunities that in 1853 he was elected to Congress. One term of
service in this august body was sufficient to convince Tweed
that Washington was not the sphere of activity for which he
was suited, and at the end of his two years he returned from
the temptations of the national capital rich in political experience but decidedly poorer in pocket. The flesh-pots of the
city administration had therefore greater attractions for him
than before, and in 1857 he became public school commissioner. By a judicious use of the "influence" attaching to his
position, he succeeded in getting himself elected a member of
the newly-established Board of Supervisors. He soon became
the leader of this board and was four times elected its president. This position gave him a vast amount of "influence"
which he continued to use for his own advantage until the
board was abolished in 1870.

Tweed was not the only "new man" who was emerging
from obscurity into power during this period. Among the
other "rising" men of the time were A. Oakey Hall, Peter B.
Sweeny, and Richard B. Connolly. Hall was of better birth
than the rest, and had considerable literary ability, of which he
was inordinately proud. Under an appearance of artless simpli-
city he concealed a great ambition. Though generally supposed
to occupy a somewhat higher moral plane than his associates,
he was never considered remarkable for the severity of his
principles. Sweeny was the great schemer of the "ring." He
began his public career as a "lobbyist" at Albany, and there
acquired the knowledge of men and tact in managing them for
which he was famous, and which was the means of his participation in the operations of the "Ring." Connolly was the least
attractive of all these men. He had few redeeming traits. He
was regarded as cowardly and disloyal. His important political
position was due to his talent for finance, which was considerable — greater indeed, it was thought, than his honesty. This
was always distrusted; and to this fact was due the nickname
of "Slippery Dick," frequently applied to him in the papers of
the day. For a long time these four men worked separately;
but in the end their community of aim and of methods
brought them together and "they became firmly leagued in the
pursuit of the same brilliant prize — the control of the municipal government and patronage of New York."

They undertook to win this prize by obtaining control of
the "foreign vote," *i.e.* the foreign-born population of the city,
which in the years immediately preceding 1860 had increased
enormously. In this foreign-born population the most numerous and most manageable element was the Irish. The Democratic party had always held the bulk of the Irish vote, and the
"regular" Democratic organization in the city was Tammany
Hall. The prime aim of Tweed and his associates, therefore,
was to obtain control of Tammany. . . .

In 1863 Tweed was made the chairman of the general
committee of Tammany Hall, and in the same year the grand
sachem of the Tammany Society. He was thus the official head

Engraving by Thomas Nast, published in Harper's Weekly, August 19, 1871, p. 764. Photo courtesy Chicago Historical Society.

both of the society at large and of the political organization....

It might be thought that the powers possessed by the Ring were sufficient to enable them to carry out any scheme that they had devised already or could invent in the future for the plundering of the city; but they were not yet content. The elections of 1869 had given the Democratic party a majority in both houses of the State legislature, and the Ring seized this opportunity to introduce certain changes into the city charter. These changes, though made in the immediate interest of the Ring, were for the most part sound and wise, according in principle with the most advanced modern theory of municipal administration. They tended to give the city greater power over its own local affairs, to simplify its extremely complex administrative institutions, and to centre the responsibility for the administration of local business in very few hands....

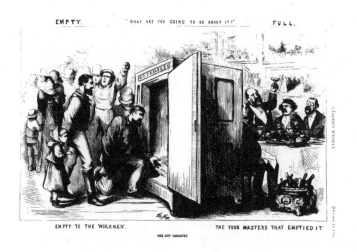

EMPTY.   "WHAT ARE YOU GOING TO DO ABOUT IT?"   FULL.

EMPTY TO THE WORKMEN.   THE FOUR MASTERS THAT EMPTIED IT

THE CITY TREASURY.

The methods which the Ring adopted to fill the pockets of its members were various in kind and of different degrees of immorality. They ran along the gamut of public dishonesty from abuse of official position for the advancement of private ends to transactions which can with difficulty be distinguished from actual theft. . . .

But all the other enterprises of the Ring dwindle into insignificance when compared with the colossal frauds that were committed in the building of the new court-house for the county. When this undertaking was begun, it was stipulated that its total cost should not exceed $250,000; but before the Ring was broken up, upwards of $8,000,000 had been expended, and the work was not completed. Here the operations of the Ring can with difficulty be distinguished from ordinary theft. Whenever a bill was brought in by one of the contractors, he was directed to increase largely the total of his charge; and it was difficult, if not impossible, for him to get his pay if he did not comply. The usual result of course was compliance. A warrant was then drawn for the amount of the bill as raised; the contractor was paid, perhaps the amount of his original bill, perhaps a little more; and the difference between the original and the raised bills was divided between the members of the Ring. It is said that about sixty-five percent of the bills actually paid by the county represented fraudulent addition of this sort. The Ring was fairly safe from scrutiny or control because all the county offices which had been established to supervise and check the payments from the public treasury were filled by its agents. Tweed, in his capacity as commissioner, would order the work to be done; by means of his influence in the board of supervisors, of which it will be remembered he was the president, he would have the bills passed: Watson, the county auditor, Tweed's tool and accomplice, would approve them, and the warrants of payment would then be issued. In order to prevent the people from knowing how much of their money was being spent, Comptroller Connolly withheld . . . the report on the finances of the city and county, which he was legally bound to make on the first day of January, and rendered no report until October. In this report everything of a suspicious character was placed in an account called "general purposes." In the meantime, notwithstanding an enormous increase in the taxes, the city debt was increasing at a rate which would have excited general alarm had the people known the facts. . . .

The following figures will give an approximate idea of the amount the Ring cost the city of New York. In 1860, before Tweed came into power, the debt of the city was reported as amounting only to $20,000,000 while the tax rate was about 1.60 percent on the assessed valuation of the property in the city liable to taxation. In the middle of the year 1871, the total debt of the city and the county — which were coterminous, and for all practical purposes the same — amounted to $100,955,333.33, and the tax rate had risen to over 2 percent. During the last two years and a half of the government of the Ring the debt increased at the rate of $28,652,000 a year. . . .

The old party system still remains and must, in a large city like New York with its great masses of ignorant voters, ever offer a great obstacle to the selection of the best men for office. The radical changes now advocated in the methods of elections, and the reform of the civil service by the extension of competitive examinations, can only serve as palliatives. Many of the evils which the city has experienced in the past may be expected to recur, until such time as its electors are more intelligent, their allegiance to party less strong, and their political leaders more pure.

The Immigrant & the Boss

During the nineteenth century, New York City grew from a modest sized urban community to the largest metropolis in the nation. Immigrants from England, Ireland, Germany, and eastern Europe flocked to her neighborhoods. Nearly half of New York's 1870 population consisted of Irish and German immigrants. Largely unskilled and speaking different languages, the immigrant was ill-equipped to deal with the complexities of modern urban life. Securing living quarters, finding work, or coping with new cultural patterns were frequent obstacles in the life of the newcomer. In New York, as in other cities, ethnic group associations attempted to provide services to ease the adjustment pains. Lacking political power and a source of funding, these groups proved incapable of resolving the immigrant's difficulties.

The political boss stepped in to provide the services needed by the immigrants. From the time of Tweed's rule until the 1930's, immigrant groups consistently voted to return the boss to office. The tie between the political machine and the immigrant was equally strong over the last 100 years in Pittsburgh, Cincinnati, Chicago, Boston, and Kansas City.

*In the following essay, Alexander Callow examines the
relationship between Tweed's machine and the immigrants. He
demonstrates that Tweed offered needed services to immigrants and thereby challenges the harsh views expressed by
Frank Goodnow in the previous selection.*

The nineteenth-century immigrant was the disinherited of a
new frontier. For thousands of them the frontier was not the
wild, untamed wilderness and the hostile Indian. Their frontier
was the city, where the dangers of the forest were substituted
by exploitation by political machines. They faced the contempt of oldtimers — the rooted, established "native" American — and were forced to endure all the painful unexpected
adjustments to American urban life. For some the new frontier
meant a rebirth, a rich existence filled with opportunities
unequaled in the Old World; for others it meant an existence
of frustration and poverty, where the promise of American
life ironically seemed closed to them. The growth of modern
urban political machines, whether under the Tweed Ring or
later machines in New York, was in large part determined by
the adjustment of the immigrant to the city.

. . . Political upheavals and the great potato famines of
1846-48, which struck both Ireland and Germany, created for
thousands a desperate need to flee to the New World. To use
Oscar Handlin's words, "these people had no choice of destina-
tion. They were almost unique in the history of immigration in
their intense desire to flee to America." As opposed to the
immigrants before the 1840's, they lacked skill and capital
which made it extremely difficult for them to move beyond
the city; indeed, the greater number had to remain in New
York. . . .

The bulk of the immigrants found themselves painfully
ill-equipped to survive in the new urban world. Landless pea-

sants, rooted in a profoundly static rural environment, they found the skilled, specialized middle-class occupations closed to them. For most, only the more menial, dirty, poorly paying jobs were available. The women went into domestic service, and some — to prostitution. The men worked on the docks, swept the streets, or hired out as laborers in the building trades. For the politically inclined, especially the Irish, the saloon, the police force, and the fire companies served them.

The newcomer found that he had escaped the poverty of the farm to find the poverty of the city. His home was that well-known New York eyesore, the tenement. His existence was barely marginal. His daily life was a constant harassment of a lack of water, sewage, ventilation, sanitation — and respect. Filth, disease, periodic unemployment, family disorganization, and despair, erupted into what particularly worried the native middle classes — disorder and crime. . . .

Buffeted by the distrust of the native and the challenge of the city, the immigrant joined his own kind in order to grapple with the pressures and anxieties of his life. By settling in ethnic clusters the immigrants gave the city on the East and West Sides the appearance of a collection of little "Europes." But this kind of solidarity by no means suggested that the immigrants had shut themselves off from American life. As one historian has noted with excellent insight, the immigrants "reflected widespread acceptance of the common middle-class ideals dominant in the society about them. Even the mass of former peasants, who could not in their own lives apply the American axioms of thrift, hard work, advancement, and progress, recognized that these were the keys to respect and status in the United States."

Tammany Hall, with motives more expedient than altruistic, seeing the immigrants confronted with and often confounded by the hard problems of the city, came to their aid. While reformers preached about civic responsibility, efficiency in government, and particularly lower taxes, Tammany exchanged cheer, charity, and jobs for votes. The Tweed Ring learned the art of being ethnic brokers. When the steamers came in, Democrats flocked to Castle Gardens to offer the immigrant a bowl of soup, guide him to a cheap boarding house, and often find him a job. Tammany and its many affiliated ward clubs provided good fellowship, which usually revolved around the bar, where the newcomer could find a sympathetic ear for his resentments. Here, too, Tammany could strengthen group-consciousness by appealing to the immigrants' national pride. For example, on December 29, 1870, at a Democratic General Committee meeting, Grand Sachem Tweed presiding, Richard O'Gorman, who was not only an eloquent Irishman but also Corporation Counsel for the City of New York, offered these resolutions.

> The Democratic Party never fails to sympathize with all men who devote themselves to the cause of their country's independence, and
>
> Whereas, Certain Irishmen who have suffered painful imprisonment in various British prisons and were punished for their opposition to British dominion in Ireland, have been recently released and are expected soon to arrive in the City of New York; therefore;
>
> Resolved, That the General Committee of the Tammany Society, pledged as it is to the cause of freedom all over the world, tender to the Irish patriots a cordial welcome.

The Boss himself began the celebration by giving $1000.

The generosity of the beneficent Tweed, however, should not belie the fact that Tammany ruthlessly exploited the immigrant. The fundamental interests of Tammany were not those of the immigrant but the cold, calculated pursuance of the narrow self-interests of Tammany Hall. If this coincided with the interests of the immigrants, all well and good; if not, the immigrant was either ignored or shunted aside. More often than not, the two interests did not coincide. Conservative Tammany Hall never undertook a sustained attack on the critical ills affecting the newcomer — poverty, housing, educa-

tion, etc. Charity and patronage were doled out in bits and
pieces for the purpose of strengthening the political position
of the Tweed Ring's Tammany organization. Nor did the
immigrant fare much better in other cities under different
regimes, such as the venal Republican machine in Philadelphia.

To satisfy their need for campanionship and organization,
the immigrants formed mutual-aid societies, churches, newspapers, theaters, militia, and fire companies, many of which
could provide strong political support. Politics offered one of
the very few escapes from Wooster or Water streets, and
Tammany enrolled the Irish and the Germans into the district
organizations, rewarding zeal with a committee post and a
public office. In the 1850's Fernando Wood made New York's
"finest" into an institution to win immigrant favor and dispense patronage. . . .

The Tweed Ring shrewdly went much beyond Wood and
opened up an unusually large number of public offices to the
Germans and the Irish. Indeed the Ring used the immigrant to
help create the first modern city machine in New York and to
streamline Tammany Hall. Never before had the Democratic
party so effectively gained the support of the newcomer. The
Tweed Ring provided an unprecedented number of jobs for
immigrants. This is not to say, as it has been argued, that the
Tweed days mark the coming of the immigrants, especially the
Irish, into his own, politically. True, the Irish were infiltrating
almost every branch of government; true, the old Anglo-Saxon
ruling class was leaving politics for industry and finance, and
more and more Irish filled their places. But if the ethnic
character of political leadership is any criterion, two Ringmen,
Tweed and Hall, were of Scottish and English origin respective-
ly, and the first Irish Catholic city boss did not emerge until
John Kelly, after the Ring's fall. The Tweed era, therefore,
marks a transitional stage which would culminate in Irish
domination of Tammany Hall and New York City politics. . . .

———————— ◆ ◆◆ ◆◆ ◆ ————————

The immigrant needed time to shed his European heritage.

Coming from a peasant environment, often ruled by an autoc-
racy, he was bewildered and alienated by the Yankee-
Protestant notion of politics. He could be led by the Tweed
Ring and later city bosses because in the past he had been led
by one "boss" or another — the landowner, royalty, the
aristocracy. Politics to him meant not some misty goal of
high-sounding principles, but something that would specifically advance his welfare. An anti-immigrant spokesman would
say, "The immigrant lacks the faculty of abstraction. He
thinks not of the welfare of the community but only of
himself." As Oscar Handlin points out, "it never occurred to
this critic that precious little thought was given by others to
the welfare of the newcomers." Used to the paternalism of the
Old World, he sought improvement through personal contacts
and personal loyalties, something the Tweed Ring understood
and exploited. The reformer simply could not break the communication barrier. When an "honest" man came among the
citizens of the lower wards, speaking of temperance, Sabbatar-
ianism, civic responsibility, the evils of patronage, the neces-
sity of justice, and the logic of economy, the immigrant's
reaction was one of suspicion and fear. The cry for efficiency
and the end of patronage might mean the end of his job.
Economy might scotch the building of a new school for his
child. To him civic responsibility was an understanding of his
plight, justice was a playground for the children, or something
to eat when times were bad. With a certain qualification, not
abstractions but basic needs were the critical issues of politics.

The qualification was that Tammany was not altogether
above using abstractions. It is well known that Tammany used
the devices of food, a job, and coal to win immigrant support.
But it has not always been realized that Tammany used an
abstraction, an idea that persuasively caught the minds and
imaginations of newcomers — the abstraction of patriotism. It
was heady stuff for the new immigrants after the 1840's
because of their urgent compulsion to be a part of America, on
one hand, and because of the constant ridicule and contempt
of nativists on the other, who held that the immigrant was a

threat to American ideals. Patriotism became a means for the newcomer to prove himself worthy, and Tammany Hall was the Pied Piper leading him on. . . .

For all the exaggerations, no matter how much Tammany's motives for patriotism may be questioned, the super-patriotic appeal was an effective force in cementing the new-comer to the leadership of New York's Democratic party. The Tweed Ring controlled an organization that had from the very beginning posed as a patriotic society. To be sure it was an organization concerned not with the larger issues of national policy, but committed totally to advancing its own self-interest in the City and State of New York. But on national holidays or on days commemorating some heroic American achievement, Tammany reacted with the highest degree of patriotic fervor and purple prose. . . .

Tammany's nationalism was not a unique departure from practical politics, but rather a marrying of patriotism and politics to achieve local, practical ends. In effect, Tammany assumed the role of spokesman for American ideals. For the immigrant especially, it posed as the machinery behind the Americanization process. The Tweed Ring accepted and accel-erated this tradition. It made Tammany the guardian of the ideals of American life so urgently sought by the newcomer. It combined the old traditions of Tammany — patriotism and anti-aristocratic appeals — with the ideals of the day: equal rights, free opportunity, free public schools, religious freedom — to be achieved, of course, only by following the guiding hand of St. Tammany. It exploited the immigrants' frustra-tions and despair and created, as it were, a politics of resent-ment. Enemies of Tammany and reformers in general were identified as the opponents of true patriotism and American ideals, and the source of all the immigrants' woes. All this plus free lodges, free cigars on election day, free coal in the winter, a bail bond when in trouble, a kind word at a wake, and a job, proved irresistible to the immigrant and the native poor alike.

These appeals to patriotism were artfully combined with unflinching attention to the grass-roots of immigrant life. This

approach represented a kind of revolution in New York politics. Prior to the reign of Fernando Wood, political factions
were controlled by men belonging to the upper or middle
class, who tended to see politics as a duty, not a profession.
From the days of Tweed's Forty Thieves through the Civil
War, a change was gradually occurring beneath the surface of
political life. The old ruling groups, even the august Albany
Regency, were being slowly displaced by a group not new, but
different in numbers and the ranks from which it came, the
professional politicians. As New York itself grew, politics
became more centralized, more disciplined, more professional-
ized. It became more of a business, and despite the schemes of
the Tweed Ring, not always a dirty business. It involved also
the everyday routine of building an organization and a following, the often dreary, exhausting leg work of politics, which
did not appeal to the "respectabilities." As the old ruling class
abdicated from practical politics, visiting the lower wards only
to deliver lofty moral manifestoes, the professionals moved in.
Professionalization meant new opportunities for ex-firemen
like Tweed or a poor boy like Sweeny, who would have found
it difficult to compete with the gentry in former days. Impor-
tantly, it meant that the native-born Tweeds and Sweenys, the
fagged-out symbols of respectability like Hall, the lawyers,
doctors, merchant princes, shopkeepers, scions of old families
– the old ruling groups – had to begin to move over and make
a place for a new group, the Connollys – the Irish immigrant.

Tweed, Sweeny, and Connolly understood this. They
studied the immigrants' ways, attended their weddings and
funerals, participated in their club life, became specialists in
personal relations and personal loyalties. Politics was a business, not business efficiency which often expressed itself in an
inhuman regard for the individual, but the business of
getting votes. Tweed understood this when in the winter of
1870 he gave $50,000 to the Seventh Ward to buy food and
coal, something the reformers never understood. Nor would
they understand how professional politicians made politics a
thing of good fellowship – indeed fun – like an exciting

"WHAT ARE YOU LAUGHING AT? TO THE VICTOR BELONG THE SPOILS."

torchlight parade for Tweed, Mike Norton treating 1500 supporters to a clambake, Slippery Dick Connolly's annual ward club ball. And certainly the do-gooders would find only contempt for this Irish drinking song:

A short time ago a gentleman named Darrity
Was elected to the Senate by a very large majority
He was so elated that he went to Dennis Cassity
Who owns a saloon of a very large capacity
He said to Dennis, "Just send out to a brewer
And get a hundred kegs of beer and give it to the poor
Then send out to a butcher shop and get a hundred tons of
    meat
And then ask the boys and girls to come and have a bite to eat
Send out invitations in a hundred different languages
And tell 'em to come and have a glass of beer and sandwiches."

Thus the immigrants, undergoing a painful adjustment to American life, frustrated by the terrible realities of the city, alienated from the reformers, transferred their Old World loyalties to the professional politicians, who, while exploiting them, at least understood them. In the heavily-immigrant Seventh Ward the loyalty remained to the very end. In November of 1871, when the Tweed Ring was rapidly falling apart and the Boss was indicted a month earlier for fraud, when it was evident that the city had been looted, the Seventh Ward re-elected William Marcy Tweed to the State Senate. The reformers found it incomprehensible and paid the price for ignoring the newcomer. But the immigrants of Tweed's ward remembered the food, the jobs, the money offered in hard times, the compassionate interests in their problems. It was to the Boss that they gave the "last hurrah."

The Ward Boss

To maintain effective communication with the varying
ethnic and racial groups within the city, political machines
placed great emphasis on neighborhood control. Each political
division of the city, the ward, had its own political leader. The
ward boss distributed services to those in need, maintained
effective communications between the party boss and the
voters and insured a large voting turnout on election day.
George Washington Plunkitt operated as a ward boss in New
York City for over thirty years. In the following selections,
Plunkitt describes the nature of his job, his relationship with
the people of the ward and his rationale for the corruption of
machine politicians. Considering the essential services rendered
by the machine, was corruption a just price?

There's thousands of young men in this city who will go to
the polls for the first time next November. Among them will
be many who have watched the careers of successful men in

Reprinted from William L. Riordan (ed.), *Plunkitt of Tammany Hall*
(New York: Alfred Knopf, 1948), pp. 3-8; 9-14; 36-38; 123-126.

politics, and who are longin' to make names and fortunes for themselves at the same game. It is to these youths that I want to give advice. First, let me say that I am in a position to give what the courts call expert testimony on the subject. I don't think you can easily find a better example than I am of success in politics. After forty years' experience at the game I am — well, I'm George Washington Plunkitt. Everybody knows what figure I cut in the greatest organization on earth, and if you hear people say that I've laid away a million or so since I was a butcher's boy in Washington Market, don't come to me for an indignant denial. I'm pretty comfortable, thank you.

Now, havin' qualified as an expert, as the lawyers say, I am goin' to give advice free to the young men who are goin' to cast their first votes, and who are lookin' forward to political glory and lots of cash. Some young men think they can learn how to be successful in politics from books, and they cram their heads with all sorts of college rot. They couldn't make a bigger mistake. Now, understand me, I ain't sayin' nothin' against colleges. I guess they'll have to exist as long as there's bookworms, and I suppose they do some good in a certain way, but they don't count in politics. In fact, a young man who has gone through the college course is handicapped at the outset. He may succeed in politics, but the chances are 100 to 1 against him.

Another mistake: some young men think that the best way to prepare for the political game is to practise speakin' and becomin' orators. That's all wrong. We've got some orators in Tammany Hall, but they're chiefly ornamental. You never heard of Charlie Murphy delivering a speech, did you? Or Richard Croker, or John Kelly, or any other man who has been a real power in the organization? Look at the thirty-six district leaders of Tammany Hall to-day. How many of them travel on their tongues? Maybe one or two, and they don't count when business is doin' at Tammany Hall. The men who rule have practised keepin' their tongues still, not exercisin' them. So you want to drop the orator idea unless you mean to go into politics just to perform the sky-rocket act.

Now, I've told you what not to do; I guess I can explain best what to do to succeed in politics by tellin' you what I did. After goin' through the apprenticeship of the business while I was a boy by workin' around the district headquarters and hustlin' about the polls on election day, I set out when I cast my first vote to win fame and money in New York city politics. Did I offer my services to the district leader as a stump-speaker? Not much. The woods are always full of speakers. Did I get up a book on municipal government and show it to the leader? I wasn't such a fool. What I did was to get some marketable goods before goin' to the leaders. What do I mean by marketable goods? Let me tell you: I had a cousin, a young man who didn't take any particular interest in politics. I went to him and said: "Tommy, I'm goin' to be a politician, and I want to get a followin'; can I count on you?" He said: "Sure, George." That's how I started in business. I got a marketable commodity — one vote. Then I went to the district leader and told him I could command two votes on election day, Tommy's and my own. He smiled on me and told me to go ahead. If I had offered him a speech or a bookful of learnin', he would have said, "Oh, forget it!"

That was beginnin' business in a small way, wasn't it? But that is the only way to become a real lastin' statesman. I soon branched out. Two young men in the flat next to mine were school friends. I went to them, just as I went to Tommy, and they agreed to stand by me. Then I had a followin' of three voters and I began to get a bit chesty. Whenever I dropped into district headquarters, everybody shook hands with me, and the leader one day honored me by lightin' a match for my cigar. And so it went on like a snowball rollin' down a hill. I worked the flat-house that I lived in from the basement to the top floor, and I got about a dozen young men to follow me. Then I tackled the next house and so on down the block and around the corner. Before long I had sixty men back of me, and formed the George Washington Plunkitt Association.

What did the district leader say then when I called at headquarters? I didn't have to call at headquarters. He came

after me and said: "George, what do you want? If you don't
see what you want, ask for it. Wouldn't you like to have a job
or two in the departments for your friends?" I said: "I'll think
it over; I haven't yet decided what the George Washington
Plunkitt Association will do in the next campaign." You ought
to have seen how I was courted and petted then by the leaders
of the rival organizations. I had marketable goods and there
was bids for them from all sides, and I was a risin' man in
politics. As time went on, and my association grew, I thought I
would like to go the Assembly. I just had to hint at what I
wanted, and three different organizations offered me the nomination. Afterwards, I went to the Board of Aldermen, then to
the State Senate, then became leader of the district, and so on
up and up till I became a statesman.

That is the way and the only way to make a lastin' success
in politics. If you are goin' to cast your first vote next
November and want to go into politics, do as I did. Get a
followin', if it's only one man, and then go the district leader
and say: "I want to join the organization. I've got one man
who'll follow me through thick and thin." The leader won't
laugh at your one-man followin'. He'll shake your hand
warmly, offer to propose you for membership in his club, take
you down to the corner for a drink and ask you to call again.
But go to him and say: "I took first prize at college in
Aristotle; I can recite all Shakespeare forwards and backwards;
there ain't nothin' in science that ain't as familiar to me as
blockades on the elevated roads and I'm the real thing in the
way of silver-tongued orators." What will he answer? He'll
probably say: "I guess you are not to blame for your misfor-
tunes, but we have no use for you here."

Plunkitt describes how one maintains control of a ward.

What tells in holdin' your grip on your district is to go right
down among the poor families and help them in the different
ways they need help. I've got a regular system for this. If
there's a fire in Ninth, Tenth, or Eleventh Avenue, for example, any hour of the day or night, I'm usually there with

some of my election district captains as soon as the fire-engines. If a family is burned out I don't ask whether they are Republicans or Democrats, and I don't refer them to the Charity Organization Society, which would investigate their case in a month or two and decide they were worthy of help about the time they are dead from starvation. I just get quarters for them, buy clothes for them if their clothes were burned up, and fix them up till they get things runnin' again. It's philanthropy, but it's politics, too — mighty good politics. Who can tell how many votes one of these fires bring me? The poor are the most grateful people in the world, and, let me tell you, they have more friends in their neighborhoods than the rich have in theirs.

If there's a family in my district in want I know it before the charitable societies do, and me and my men are first on the ground. I have a special corps to look up such cases. The consequence is that the poor look up to George W. Plunkitt as a father, come to him in trouble — and don't forget him on election day.

Another thing, I can always get a job for a deservin' man. I make it a point to keep on the track of jobs, and it seldom happens that I don't have a few up my sleeve ready for use. I know every big employer in the district and in the whole city, for that matter, and they ain't in the habit of sayin' no to me when I ask them for a job.

And the children — the little roses of the district! Do I forget them? Oh, no! They know me, every one of them, and they know that a sight of Uncle George and candy means the same thing. Some of them are the best kind of vote-getters. I'll tell you a case. Last year a little Eleventh Avenue rosebud whose father is a Republican, caught hold of his whiskers on election day and said she wouldn't let go till he'd promise to vote for me. And she didn't.

Plunkitt describes the normal working day of a ward boss.

2 a.m.: Aroused from sleep by the ringing of his door bell; went to the door and found a bartender, who asked him to go

to the police station and bail out a saloon-keeper who had been arrested for violating the excise law. Furnished bail and returned to bed at three o'clock.

6 a.m.: Awakened by fire engines passing his house. Hastened to the scene of the fire, according to the custom of the Tammany district leaders, to give assistance to the fire sufferers, if needed. Met several of his election district captains who are always under orders to look out for fires, which are considered great vote-getters. Found several tenants who had been burned out, took them to a hotel, supplied them with clothes, fed them, and arranged temporary quarters for them until they could rent and furnish new apartments.

8:30 a.m.: Went to the police court to look after his constituents. Found six "drunks." Secured the discharge of four by a timely word with the judge, and paid the fines of two.

9 a.m.: Appeared in the Municipal District Court. Directed one of his district captains to act as counsel for a widow against whom dispossession proceedings had been instituted and obtained an extension of time. Paid the rent of a poor family about to be dispossessed and gave them a dollar for food.

11 a.m.: At home again. Found four men waiting for him. One had been discharged by the Metropolitan Railway Company for neglect of duty, and wanted the district leader to fix things. Another wanted a job on the road. The third sought a place on the Subway and the fourth, a plumber, was looking for work with the Consolidated Gas Company. The district leader spent nearly three hours fixing things for the four men and succeeded in each case.

3 p.m.: Attended the funeral of an Italian as far as the ferry. Hurried back to make his appearance at the funeral of a Hebrew constituent. Went conspicuously to the front booth in the Catholic church and the synagogue, and later attended the Hebrew confirmation ceremonies in the synagogue.

7 p.m.: Went to district headquarters and presided over a meeting of election district captains. Each captain submitted a

list of all the voters in his district, reported on their attitude toward Tammany, suggested who might be won over and how they could be won, told who were in need, and who were in trouble of any kind and the best way to reach them. District leader took notes and gave orders.

8 p.m.: Went to a church fair. Took chances on everything, bought ice-cream for the young girls and the children. Kissed the little ones, flattered their mothers and took their fathers out for something down at the corner.

9 p.m.: At the club-house again. Spent $10 on tickets for a church excursion and promised a subscription for a new church-bell. Bought tickets for a baseball game to be played by two nines from his district. Listened to the complaints of a dozen push-cart peddlers who said they were persecuted by the police and assured them he would go to the Police Headquarters in the morning and see about it.

10:30 p.m.: Attended a Hebrew wedding reception and dance. Had previously sent a handsome wedding present to the bride.

12 p.m.: In bed.

Plunkitt raises the question, what is graft?
Everybody is talkin' these days about Tammany men growin' rich on graft, but nobody thinks of drawin' the distinction between honest graft and dishonest graft. There's all the difference in the world between the two. Yes, many of our men have grown rich in politics. I have myself. I've made a big fortune out of the game, and I'm gettin' richer every day, but I've not gone in for dishonest graft – blackmailin' gamblers, saloon-keepers, disorderly people, etc. – and neither has any of the men who have made big fortunes in politics.

There's an honest graft, and I'm an example of how it works. I might sum up the whole thing by sayin': "I seen my opportunities and I took 'em."

Just let me explain by examples. My party's in power in the city, and it's goin' to undertake a lot of public improvements.

Well, I'm tipped off, say, that they're going to lay out a new park at a certain place.

I see my opportunity and I take it. I go to that place and I buy up all the land I can in the neighborhood. Then the board of this or that makes its plan public, and there is a rush to get my land, which nobody cared particular for before.

Ain't it perfectly honest to charge a good price and make a profit on my investment and foresight? Of course, it is. Well, that's honest graft.

Or supposin' it's a new bridge they're goin' to build. I get tipped off and I buy as much property as I can that has to be taken for approaches. I sell at my own price later on and drop some more money in the bank.

Wouldn't you? It's just like lookin' ahead in Wall Street or in the coffee or cotton market. It's honest graft, and I'm lookin' for it every day in the year. I will tell you frankly that I've got a good lot of it, too.

I'll tell you of one case. They were goin' to fix up a big park, no matter where. I got on to it, and went lookin' about for land in that neighborhood.

I could get nothin' at a bargain but a big piece of swamp, but I took it fast enough and held on to it. What turned out was just what I counted on. They couldn't make the park complete without Plunkitt's swamp, and they had to pay a good price for it. Anything dishonest in that?

Up in the watershed I made some money, too. I bought up several bits of land there some years ago and made a pretty good guess that they would be bought up for water purposes later by the city.

Somehow, I always guessed about right, and shouldn't I enjoy the profit of my foresight? It was rather amusin' when the condemnation commissioners came along and found piece after piece of the land in the name of George Plunkitt of the Fifteenth Assembly District, New York City. They wondered how I knew just what to buy. The answer is — I seen my opportunity and I took it. I haven't confined myself to land; anything that pays is in my line.

For instance, the city is repavin' a street and has several hundred thousand old granite blocks to sell. I am on hand to buy, and I know just what they are worth.

How? Never mind that. I had a sort of monopoly of this business for a while, but once a newspaper tried to do me. It got some outside men to come over from Brooklyn and New Jersey to bid against me.

Was I done? Not much. I went to each of the men and said: "How many of these 250,000 stones do you want?" One said 20,000, and another wanted 15,000, and another wanted 10,000. I said: "All right, let me bid for the lot, and I'll give each of you all you want for nothin'."

They agreed, of course. Then the auctioneer yelled: "How much am I bid for these 250,000 fine pavin' stones?"

"Two dollars and fifty cents," says I.

"Two dollars and fifty cents!" screamed the auctioneer. "Oh, that's a joke! Give me a real bid."

He found the bid was real enough. My rivals stood silent. I got the lot for $2.50 and gave them their share. That's how the attempt to do Plunkitt ended, and that's how all such attempts end.

I've told you how I got rich by honest graft. Now, let me tell you that most politicians who are accused of robbin' the city get rich the same way.

They didn't steal a dollar from the city treasury. They just seen their opportunities and took them. That is why, when a reform administration comes in and spends a half million dollars in tryin' to find the public robberies they talked about in the campaign, they don't find them.

The books are always all right. The money in the city treasury is all right. Everything is all right. All they can show is that the Tammany heads of departments looked after their friends, within the law, and gave them what opportunities they could to make honest graft. Now, let me tell you that's never goin' to hurt Tammany with the people. Every good man looks after his friends, and any man who doesn't isn't likely to be popular. If I have a good thing to hand out in private life, I give it to a friend. Why shouldn't I do the same in public life?

Another kind of honest graft. Tammany has raised a good many salaries. There was an awful howl by the reformers, but don't you know that Tammany gains ten votes for every one it lost by salary raisin'?

The Wall Street banker thinks it shameful to raise a department clerk's salary from $1500 to $1800 a year, but every man who draws a salary himself says: "That's all right. I wish it was me." And he feels very much like votin' the Tammany ticket on election day, just out of sympathy.

Tammany was beat in 1901 because the people were deceived into believin' that it worked dishonest graft. They didn't draw a distinction between dishonest and honest graft, but they saw that some Tammany men grew rich, and supposed they had been robbin' the city treasury or levyin' blackmail on disorderly houses, or workin' in with the gamblers and lawbreakers.

As a matter of policy, if nothing else, why should the Tammany leaders go into such dirty business, when there is so much honest graft lyin' around when they are in power? Did you ever consider that?

Now, in conclusion, I want to say that I don't own a dishonest dollar. If my worst enemy was given the job of writin' my epitaph when I'm gone, he couldn't do more than write:

"George W. Plunkitt. He Seen His Opportunities, and He Took 'Em."

Corporations, Machines & Bosses

While the preceding essays seem to suggest that bosses depended almost exclusively upon the support of immigrant groups, no political machine could have extended its power without active compliance from many other segments of the community. The emerging industrial corporation of the late nineteenth century formed close relationships with bosses in order to obtain legal and economic advantages. Corporations desired the lucrative contracts for providing city services such as lighting and transportation. Because many firms competed for these economic prizes, the political machines had a ready source of graft and corruption. Political machines also had a great need for money to pay its workers and provide social services to immigrant groups. In the following selection, Mosei Ostrogorski provides an early analysis of the tie between corporations and the political machine.

The direct exploitation of municipal interests, on the brutal methods popularized by Tweed, was at an early stage supple-

Reprinted from M. Ostrogorski: *Democracy and the Organization of Political Parties*, Volume II. Translated from the French by Frederick Clarke, (New York, Macmillan, 1902), pp. 177-180; 424-428.

mented, and afterwards more and more replaced, by indirect
exploitation. This last method was peculiarly favoured by a
special phenomenon of the economic expansion, the stimu-
lating property of which in the corruption of municipal government I have already pointed out. The special economic
factor referred to was the rise of joint-stock industrial con-
cerns, of corporations. While imparting to corruption a fresh
development, often of a more subtle but of an exceedingly
penetrating kind, it enabled the party Organization at the same
time to take a more direct, more personal share in the prostitution of the powers of government to private interests. The
extraordinary outburst of manufactures and of speculation,
after the war, brought about a concentration of capital unprecedented in history, which made a comparatively limited
number of capitalist combinations masters of most of the
economic functions of the country. Daily spreading further
and further, the companies overran the American continent all
the more easily that the notions and the habits of individual
freedom and non-intervention of the State, which had passed
into dogmas, secured industrial liberty, and that the legislator
trained in these notions and habits was taken unawares by the
unexpected evolution of industrial relations. While rendering
great services to the community and developing its economic
life with increasing force and rapidity, the corporations exhibited insatiable greed and, as it were, an innate tendency to
push their way by trampling on individual interests, or on the
weaker interests which crossed their path. They tried to create
monopolies by crushing competition *per fas et nefas*. Will the
State remain a passive spectator of this power, or will it use its
authority to arrest this coalition of selfish interests, which in
their career of encroachment may constitute a danger for the
general interest, or in any event will it be watchful enough to
stop direct usurpation on their part? These were the questions
raised from the very beginning. The answer given by the course
of events was not satisfactory; the organs of government
showed themselves at the outset indifferent or even too
obliging to the corporations. With culpable complaisance they

made over to the companies large portions of the public
property entrusted to their care, and by their tolerance facilitated the abuses in which the latter indulged. The corporations, which had command of money, used it lavishly to buy
the support and the connivance of which they stood in need.

Their operations were directed in the first place against
municipal administration, with a view to obtaining from it
concessions which consisted of the right to run undertakings
of public interest, to utilize the public thoroughfares or the
land of the city for street-cars, railways, railroads in transit, gas
works, electrical supply, water works, etc. These concessions
or "franchises," out of which the companies made a profit,
consequently represented for the cities which had the disposal
of them an asset for which it was only right to obtain a return.
But the companies more often than not managed to get the
franchises gratis, or by payment of an absurdly small due; they
bought the members of the city councils, which were generally
filled, thanks to the Caucus, with politicians of a low stamp.
The steady growth of the cities and the technical improvements in the means of transport and communication increased
the number of the franchises and their value, and along with
them the opportunities for corruption. The traffic in franchises became very common in the large cities; it created a
particular species of town councillors, which acquired a melan-
choly popularity under the name of "boodle aldermen,", from
whom the corporations bought the ordinance of the council,
or who even of their own accord organized a syndicate to hold
out a public right until a purchaser could be found. The
municipal freebooters, organized in "rings" or "combines,"
thus found a means of making money without taking it directly out of the pockets of the ratepayers, but the loss was none
the less enormous to the latter; for if the companies had paid
the cities for the franchises, or paid what they were worth,
there would have been no need, as has been calculated in the
case of New York, for instance, of municipal taxes to defray
the city expenditure. The corporations obtained numberless
other favours which consolidated their monopoly, to the detri-

ment of the citizens, or even of future generations, bound by
the culpable complaisance or negligence of the municipalities.
With their complicity the corporations even evaded payment
of their proper quota of rates, and paid only a very small
portion of them, leaving the burden to be borne by the poorer
ratepayers.

While buying boodle aldermen directly whenever they
could, the companies, which had considerable interests at
stake, hit upon the plan of supplementing their resource by
trying to pack the councils in their own way and for their own
convenience, to get in men who would be at their disposal
from the beginning. With this object the corporations laid
hands on the machinery of the party Organization; they inter-
vened with their money and their creatures in the primaries
and the conventions to secure the nomination of accommo-
dating candidates, or even constructed the party Machine from
top to bottom for their own use on the method adopted, for
instance, by the Gas Ring in Philadelphia, and did as they liked
with the political Organization which distributed elective offices; or again subsidized the existing Machine, which, in
return, gave them the benefit of its influence with its nomi-
nees, on the principle of *do ut des* applied to all concerned. . . .

But why should these experts be men of the stamp of
"bosses," and how does it come about that they are able to
keep a hold on the political machinery and exploit it so easily?
What are their particular means and resources? The most
common explanation given is that the Machine disposes of a
large patronage, or, again, that it lives on rich corporations,
and that if it had not one or the other of these resources, or
both of them, it would die of inanition. This explanation is
only partly true, it only deals with the material resources.
Foremost among these, in fact, comes the patronage, the
places in the public service of the Union, of the States, and of
the municipalities; these places, supplemented by the hope of
getting them, furnish the pay for maintaining the army of
politicians who serve the Machine. The more places the boss

A POPULAR GAME: TWEED IN THE CORNER

Cartoon from Harper's Weekly, April 10, 1886.

has to distribute, the more firmly established will be his power. A city boss dreams of becoming State boss, because this last position will make him the dispenser of the State patronage and of the federal patronage. The height of the State boss's ambition is to rise to be a "president-maker," by no means in order to become mayor of the palace to the President and influence the policy of the Union, but in order to secure a preponderating voice in the distribution of the places, including those of the Cabinet. The boss lives as much on the substance of the patronage as on the prestige which the possession of it gives him; and to enjoy both, he must be the sole dispenser of patronage toward whom all eyes are turned. If it were possible to obtain a place irrespective of him, or in spite of him, he would lose caste, the discipline which he wields over his men would be relaxed, and the whole Organization would be "demoralized." The number of the places at the disposal of the Machine is constantly increased by the constituted authorities, under pressure from it. Besides the patronage improperly exploited by the party Organizations there is the patronage conceded to the parties by the law, in the form of seats on election boards. To ensure the impartiality of the proceedings of these boards, they are composed of representatives of the two principal parties, appointed by their respective

THE SPIRIT OF TWEED IS MIGHTY STILL:
" And even yet you don't know what you are going to do about it !"

Cartoon from Harper's Weekly, December 18, 1886.

Organizations and paid out of public money. In a large city like New York or Philadelphia, which has more than a thousand polling-places or thereabouts, each Organization is in a position to distribute a large sum every year on this account.

Next come the principal direct receipts of the Machine — the assessments, the contributions paid by the candidates and by the office-holders. The percentage paid by these last yields of itself considerable sums. To give an idea of them, the case may be quoted of the assessments of the municipal employees in the city of Philadelphia: levied at the rate of two per cent, they provide, out of the $4,500,000 which the city spends in salaries, $90,000 for the benefit of the Machine. The contributions of the candidates are much higher, and no elective post escapes this tribute. Even candidates for the highest judicial office are obliged to pay a large sum which, in New York, for instance, generally runs into thousands of dollars. The contributions given to the funds of the Machine by private individuals, by wealthy zealots of the party, important as they are, sink into insignificance beside those of the financial or industrial corporations, especially in the States of New York and Pennsylvania. There the corporations pay a regular tribute to the boss, as "price of the peace," that is to say, to be left in peace, to ensure themselves against the hostile designs of the legislators or of the higher executive officers. Besides this, the corporations are liable to extraordinary calls on the eve of a particularly hot election campaign, in which the Machine will have to spend a great deal. It is difficult to form an accurate idea of the amount of the contributions made by the corporations; yet some useful information on this subject may be gleaned from the following data relating to New York: this city is the seat of more than 2100 corporations subject to regulation by the law, and consequently, standing in need of "protection"; their combined capital approaches the total of $2,000,000,000; most of these companies discharge the "price of the peace," and some of them pay $50,000 a year, apart from extraordinary contributions amounting to as much as $100,000. One may also mention the income which the Machine derives from the fêtes and the entertainments which it gets up for its workers: it distributes tickets of admission at somewhat high prices, $5 or $10 each, to the officials and to other persons who are under an obligation to it, such as saloon-keepers, contractors, etc. It is a form of extortion which all these persons are obliged to submit to for the greater advantage of the Machine's exchequer.

The enormous material resources of which the Machine thus disposes are not the only foundation of its success; it

possesses also a moral stock which in fact is converted into
capital like a security into cash. This moral capital consists of
the deliberate or unconscious adhesion of the various elements
of the community. The Machine exists and works with their
consent, and by no means in spite of them. The first of these
social elements on which the Machine leans is made up of its
own servants and of its nearest adherents, of the social category which is consequently known by the name of "the
Machine element." These people work for the Machine as they
would have worked for a manufacturer, a merchant, for any
one who might have employed them. They get their living in
"practical politics," and they must do so, for does not the
wisdom of nations say: "a man cannot live on wind," "people
do not go into politics for fun." The work the men of the
Machine do for it is undeniable; the duties of a leader, of a
small precinct leader and of his lieutenants, who have to oil all
the wheels of the Machine from day to day, are by no means a
sinecure; they are extremely absorbing and keep the mind in a
constant state of tension. The work is rather dirty; this may
be, but there are so many trades which involve handling
unpleasant things; every trade has its processes, and "practical
politics" has its own; the use of these processes is not so much
a matter of ethics as of technique. "It is perfectly idle to ask
oneself if it is for good or for evil," said a member of
Tammany Hall to me, who gave me a sketch of the methods of
the Great Wigwam, "it is neither bad nor good, it is politics."
The character of the pay, which consists of "spoils," is not
objectionable either, it is almost part of the natural order of
things. When the Creator, after making the two great lights of
the day and of the night, made the two great political organizations, he ordained that they should divide the public offices
between them. It is therefore only fair that these offices
should be given to the men who have "worked" for the party,
and to them alone. It is a disregard of this truth which would
be scandalous and would constitute a danger for the public
morality, nay, even for the public order of the American
democracy. A small boss once spoke to me with bitterness of

the head bosses, who sometimes bestow places on persons who do not belong to the Organization, to the detriment of those who "do the work"; "if this goes on and becomes the general practice, we shall have a monarchy."

It is by following this train of reasoning that the men of the Machine come to consider the independent members of the party who oppose the Machines as hateable and contemptible; these citizens not only prevent them from earning their living, but even try, while posing as champions of honesty, to get hold of the offices, without having "done the work" for the party; they are therefore hypocrites, full of "humbug and cant." At the best, they are only "doctrinaires," "college professors," "star-gazers," for the government without parties which they dream of is an idea as absurd as it is flagitious. The immorality is all on the side of the "reformers," who sacrifice the interest of the party to their vanity and their ambition, who do not scruple to sow discord, whereas they, the men of the Machine, sacrifice everything to "harmony." They feel proud of being "harmonious," being quite ready to waive the other virtues. "Harmony" is for them the sum and substance of morality; it generalizes in regard to public life the sentiments of fraternity which unite the politicians in their private relations, and which assume the aspect at one time of professional solidarity, at another of personal attachment. These sentiments, therefore do not stop even at the frontiers of the parties. While fighting one another according to the rules of the game, the politicians of the rival Machines are often ready, not only to make common cause against the outsiders, but to help one another, to the detriment of their own parties. For instance, a small Republican boss, to oblige his Democratic colleague and friend, who wants to get a friend of his own, a Democratic candidate, elected to a small post, orders his men to vote for that candidate, although he is a Democrat. The considerations by which the politicians are guided in thus acting have been put into words by one of them, who said to Mr. Theodore Roosevelt, "There are no politics in politics." This enigmatic utterance meant that in the world of politicians

no heed is paid to the political conventions of society. Far
from being utterly depraved men, the politicians profess rather
a clan morality, which is often in opposition with the morality
of society at large. The Machine, however, is but strengthened
thereby: the perverted clan morality justifies the conduct and
stimulates the enthusiasm of the numerous category of those
who give their mercenary support of it.

An Apology for Bossism

"The political machine is corrupt. The boss is evil and immoral." So said cartoonist Thomas Nast and the editorial staff of the New York Times in attacking William Tweed in 1871. Their successful campaign resulted in a reform government in New York City in November of that year. Tammany Hall was swept out of office in an upsurge of moral indignation. Tweed eventually went to prison. Within a decade, however, the Democratic political machine regained control of city hall. By 1890, Richard Croker held power equal to that of Tweed himself. In this selection, Croker defends the political machine and suggests several reasons for its ability to triumph over the reformers.

No political party can with reason expect to obtain power, or to maintain itself in power, unless it be efficiently organized. Between the aggressive forces of two similar groups of ideas, one entertained by a knot of theorists, the other enunciated by a well-compacted organization, there is such a differ-

Reprinted from Richard Croker, "Tammany Hall and the Democracy," *North American Review*, 154 (1892), pp. 225-230.

ence as exists between a mob and a military battalion. The
mob is fickle, bold, and timid by turns, and even in different
portions it is at the same time swayed by conflicting emotions.
In fact, it is a mere creature of emotion, while the drilled and
compacted battalion is animated and supported by purpose
and scientific plan. It has leaders, and these leaders are known
to every man in the ranks and possess their confidence. It is
thus that a single company of infantry is able to quell almost
any popular outbreak in a city; and a regiment is completely
master of the situation, even if it be outnumbered by the
malcontents in the proportion of ten or twenty to one.

The City of New York to-day contains a political organization which, in respect of age, skillful management, unity of
purpose, devotion to correct principles, public usefulness, and
finally, success, has no superior, and, in my opinion, no equal,
in political affairs the world over. I mean the *Tammany
Democracy*. I do not propose to defend the Tammany organization; neither do I propose to defend sunrise as an exhibition
of celestial mechanics; nor a democratic form of government
as an illustration of human liberty at its best. In the campaign
of 1891 almost the only argument used by the Republicans
against the Democrats was the assertion that Flower was the
candidate of a corrupt political club, and that club was named
Tammany. Tammany was accused of every vice and crime
known to Republican orators; it was a fountain-head of corruption; it was because of it that every farmer throughout the
State could not at once pay off his mortgages; it took forty
millions annually from the citizens of New York and gave
them nothing in exchange for it. To the credit of the Democrats let us note the fact that, while this torrent of abuse was
being poured upon the heads of voters, Democrats did as the
inhabitants of Spain are said to do when the clouds are
opened, — "they let it rain." Nobody apologized for the
misdeeds of the alleged malefactor; the Democrats went before
the people on legitimate issues, and the result of the affair was
expressed in the figures, 47,937 majority. I doubt if the
Democracy would have fared anything like as well if they had

defended or apologized or explained away. "He who excuses himself accuses himself" is a time-worn proverb. They let Mr. Fassett shout himself hoarse over "Tammany corruption," and they won the victory.

In fact, such a defensive attitude would have been wholly at variance with the basis on which the Tammany Democracy acts. A well-organized political club is made for the purpose of aggressive warfare. It must move, and it must always move forward against its enemies. If it makes mistakes, it leaves them behind and goes ahead. If it is encumbered by useless baggage of half-hearted or traitorous camp-followers, it cuts them off and goes ahead. While it does not claim to be exempt from error, it does claim to be always aiming at success by proper and lawful methods, and to have the good of the general community always in view as its end of effort. Such an organization has no time or place for apologies or excuses; and to indulge in them would hazard its existence and certainly destroy its usefulness.

The city and county of New York comprise a population of nearly two millions and furnish the business arena for near-by residents who represent two millions more. The political party, then, that is uppermost in New York legislates locally for the largest municipal constituency on the planet, except one. The task is clearly one of enormous magnitude, and demands a combination of skill, enterprise, knowledge, resolution, and what is known as "executive ability," which cannot be at once made to order, and cannot be furnished by any body of theorists, no matter how full may be their pockets or how righteous may be their intentions. Since the Whig party went out of existence the Democrats have administered the affairs of New York County, rarely even losing the mayorality except on personal grounds; always having the majority in the Board of Alderman, and as a rule the Sheriff's and County Clerk's offices. And at the same time the guiding force of the New York Democracy has proceeded from the Tammany organization.

As one of the members of this organization, I simply do

what all its members are ready to do as occasion offers, and that is, to stand by its principles and affirm its record. We assert, to begin with, that its system is admirable in theory and works excellently well in practice.

Coincident with the plan that all the Assembly districts shall be thoroughly looked after by experienced leaders who are in close touch with the central committees, is the development of the doctrine that the laborer is worthy of his hire; in other words, that good work is worth paying for, and in order that it may be good must be paid for. The affairs of a vast community are to be administered. Skillful men must administer them. These men must be compensated. The principle is precisely the same as that which governs the workings of a railway, or a bank, or a factory; and it is an illustration of the operation of sophistries and unsound moralities, so much in vogue among our closet reformers, than any persons who have outgrown the kindergarten should shut their eyes to this obvious truth. Now, since there must be officials, and since these officials must be paid, and well paid, in order to insure able and constant service, why should they not be selected from the membership of the society that organizes the victories of the dominant party?

In my opinion, to ask this question is to answer it. And I add that the statement made by the enemies of Tammany that "Tammany stands by its friends," is, in fact, praise, although intended for abuse. Tammany *does* stand by its friends, and it always will until some such change occurs in human affairs as will make it praiseworthy and beneficial that a man or an association should stand by his or its enemies. We are willing to admit that the logical result of this principle of action would be that all the employees of the city government, from the Mayor to the porter who makes the fire in his office, should be members of the Tammany organization. This would not be to their discredit. And if any one of them commits a malfeasance, he is just as responsible to the *people* as though he were lifted bodily out of the "Union League" or some transient "Citizens' Reform Association," and he will at once find himself outside of the Tammany membership also.

Fearfully and wonderfully made are the tales that are sent out into the rural districts touching the evil effects of "Tammany rule." The trembling countryman on arriving in New York expects to fall into a quagmire of muddy streets, and while struggling through these quicksands he fears the bunco man on one side and the sandbagger on the other. Reaching some hotel, he counts on being murdered in his bed unless he double-lock his door. That his landlord should swindle him is a foregone conclusion. And when no adventure happens, and he reaches home in safety, he points to himself, among his neighbors, as a rare specimen of a survival of the dangers that accompany the sway of a Democratic majority in New York.

The facts are that New York is a centre to which the criminal element of the entire country gravitates, simply because it offers at once a lucrative field for crime and a safe hiding-place. Therefore, to preserve social order and "keep the peace" in New York demands more ability and more policemen than are required in country solitudes. It is safe to say that any right-minded citizen who attends to his own affairs and keeps proper company and proper hours is as safe in New York as in any part of the globe, the most violently Republican township of St. Lawrence County not excepted. Our streets are clean and are in good order as to the paving, except where certain corporations tear them up and keep their rents gaping. Our city is well watered, well lighted, and well parked. It is conceded that we have the best police and fire departments in the world. Our docks are being rapidly improved, and will compare, when completed, with the Liverpool and London docks. Our tax-rate is lower than that of dozens of other American cities whose affairs are not nearly so well administered. Nor is the tax-rate low because the assessed values are high. If any real-estate owner claims that his property is overvalued, you can silence him at once by offering to buy it at the valuation. Practical real-estate owners know that the county of New York does *not* over assess its property-owners.

That the Tammany Hall Democracy will largely aid in

organizing victory for the national ticket next November is beyond question. The national Democracy is free to choose whatever candidate it may prefer. Tammany has no desire to dictate or control the choice; its part in the conflict is to elect the candidate after he shall have been named. No matter what Republican majorities may come down to the Harlem River from the interior of the State, we propose to meet and drown them with eighty-five thousand majority from New York and Kings.

The Twentieth·Century Political Boss

Bossism & Reform

THE READINGS IN THIS SECTION concentrate on three
twentieth-century bosses: Thomas Johnson of Cleveland,
Thomas Pendergast of Kansas City, and Richard Daley of
Chicago. Although all mastered the techniques of political
organization and acquired considerable political power, none
was simply a reincarnation of William Marcy Tweed or Richard
Croker. Instead, each boss operated within the confines of
rapid social and political change which constantly altered the
practice of urban government. From the first political machine
in New York City under Boss Tweed, reform parties had
battled for control of city hall; and, in the process, they had
changed the ground rules of urban politics. In fact, over the
last hundred years most large American cities have experienced
a continuing struggle between the boss and the reformer. On
occasion that struggle switches hero and villain as in the case
of Thomas Johnson who used the techniques of power politics
to achieve significant reform. To understand boss politics in
the twentieth century, we must first explore the patterns of
urban reform.

Most urban reformers attacked bossism by attempting to

change structural defects in city governments. Their criticisms often were motivated by a class bias and a strong sense of moral superiority. The graft and corruption endemic to bossism piqued the consciences of these middle- and upper-class citizens. They objected to the bosses' utilization of immigrants and lower-class citizens whose civic ignorance made them pawns for any wily politician. Structural reformers claimed that honest and efficient government would come about only by returning power to the "best people." To the reformer the city's key problem was how to efficiently utilize scarce financial resources. Turning to the organizational model of the business corporation, these reformers believed that "good citizens" and skilled administrators could return effective government to the city.

In their efforts to achieve these goals, the reformers altered the practices of city politics. By 1900, most urban areas had obtained local control of the police, of education, and of certain taxing powers from the states. To dispel the power of political parties, reformers urged non-partisan elections of city officials. They championed the use of the secret ballot to eliminate the machine's practice of exerting personal influence on voters. The adoption of sophisticated accounting procedures increased governmental efficiency as well as plugged the holes through which the boss had siphoned money into party coffers. On both the national and local levels, civil service reforms expanded the number of city jobs requiring educational qualifications and written examinations. While these practices were intended to upgrade the quality of public servants, they were also effective in reducing the number of patronage jobs, an important aspect of the bosses' reward system.

In the early twentieth century, the adoption of the city manager and commission forms of government marked the highpoint of the structural reform movement. The commission system usually consisted of five elected commissioners, whose offices were patterned after the organization of the business corporation. Under the city manager form, the commissioners appointed a city manager who supervised all the administrative functions of the city. Many cities, at the same time, abolished the practice of ward representation in favor of at-large elections. These reforms represented the prevailing belief that good city government required efficiency experts distant from the influence of the people and political parties. Soon businessmen almost totally dominated city governments, a situation which the reformers specifically desired.

While the city manager and commission plans were never adopted in America's largest cities, structural reformers had forced the widespread use of the secret ballot, management experts, and civil service examinations. Twentieth-century bosses thus were forced to operate within a structure considerably altered since the halcyon days of Boss Tweed.

There were other reformers, less influential, who went beyond the purely structural and urged major social changes within the city. In the late nineteenth and early twentieth centuries, Mayor Hazen Pingree in Detroit, Sam "Golden Rule" Jones in Toledo, and Thomas L. Johnson in Cleveland demanded that city governments provide a healthy and meaningful life for their citizens. While structural reformers had questioned the electorate's honesty and intelligence, social reformers premised their programs on the needs of the city's disadvantaged population. They were less concerned with the political corruption at the ward level, but instead directed their attention to large corporations who escaped paying taxes or charged inflated prices for services, such as lighting and transportation, which they provided the city. Pingree and many others eventually adopted municipal ownership of city services to neutralize businesses' control of city life. Although social reformers throughout the twentieth century have been in the minority, their programs did force basic changes in city government. By the 1930's, however, neither reform group had succeeded in eliminating the conditions which periodically enabled the boss to regain power.

In the 1930's the focus of power shifted in urban politics when the federal government undertook a more active role in

the solution of urban problems. Since 1900 the city's
expanding physical boundaries had complicated already serious housing shortages and transportation problems. The
migration of nearly a million black citizens from the South
into northern industrial cities increased the social responsibili-
ties of municipal governments and aggravated an already tense
racial climate. With the Great Depression, the city's strained
economic resources snapped. The New Deal programs of
President Roosevelt belatedly recognized that the problems of
the twentieth-century city were beyond merely local solutions.
Every decade since the 1930's the federal government has
increased its economic and political role within the city. At
first reformers believed that the tie between the federal
government and the city would destroy bossism because bosses
could not control a city hall partially dependent upon the
federal government. Reformers perhaps were guilty of wishful
thinking, for bossism did not disappear. A recent study of
Pittsburgh in the 1930's indicated that New Deal legislation
actually created a powerful city machine, and in Kansas City,
Thomas J. Pendergast increased his power because of ties to
the federal government and national politics. In the late 1960's
and early 1970's, no national politician could have failed to
notice that Richard Daley was more than just a city boss, for
his influence had affected several presidential elections. After a
hundred years of constant struggle between the boss and the
reformer, one can be permitted a little skepticism when
observers mark Daley's death as the end of bossism.

The Boss as Reformer

*Thomas L. Johnson, Mayor of Cleveland from 1901 to
1909, represents both the boss and the reformer of the period.
A wealthy self-made man, Johnson earned millions of dollars
during his early life by successfully consolidating street railway
operations in Cleveland, Brooklyn, Detroit and Philadelphia
and steel mills in Johnstown, Pa., and Lorain, Ohio. Each time
Johnson sold his holdings at great profit. Financially secure by
1900, Johnson turned his business principles to the question
of political reform in Cleveland. Specifically, he vowed to
eliminate monopolies and special privileges identical to those
he formerly helped to create. Campaigning on a platform of
increased self-governing power for cities, reform of city taxes,
city ownership of utilities and more efficient government, he
defeated political boss "Honest John Farley." Once elected,
however, he relied upon machine politics and much of his
personal fortune to achieve his goals.*

*The following selection, taken from Frederick Howe's, The
Confessions of a Reformer, examines the role of Johnson as
political leader and boss in Cleveland. Howe, a great friend and
admirer of Johnson served on the Cleveland City Council and*

worked for Johnson in an effort to reform the Cleveland government.

When I heard one day that this puzzling, contradictory, much-talked-of Tom Johnson had arrived and would announce his candidacy that evening at the Hollenden House, I freed myself from engagements and was there at eight o'clock. There was a stir outside and the crowd surged in. A short, pudgy man was pushed on to the cigar-stand above me. He stood round and smiling; hands in his pockets, he looked like a boy out for a lark. Politicians shouted like mad around him; evidently they expected a "barrel" campaign.

Surely, I thought, a man of wealth and position is not going to run for mayor in this undignified way. Politics is a serious business, a crusade against politicians and spoilsmen. Tom Johnson should have had a committee of prominent citizens to wait on him and ask him to run. He should have conferred with the Municipal Association and the Chamber of Commerce. That would have given dignity to his campaign.

When the crowd grew quiet Mr. Johnson began to speak. He started in the middle of things. He had permanently given up the making of money, he said, and had come back from New York to run for mayor. He had sold out all his railways and his iron and steel plants, and intended to devote the rest of his life to politics. He talked about the city. The steam railroads had gotten possession of the lake front and held it illegally. The lake-front land was worth millions of dollars. The city was contesting the railroad occupancy in the United States courts, where the case had lain for a dozen years. Mayor Farley was attempting to jam legislation through the council to validate these illegal holdings. In addition, he was doing everything he could to give the street railways a very valuable franchise; a franchise, Mr. Johnson said, worth many millions of dollars. He knew how much it was worth, because he had been in the

Frederic C. Howe, *The Confessions of a Reformer.* (New York, 1925), pp. 88-90, 92-95, 98, 100, 108-111, 113.

street-railway business and had made millions out of just such franchise grants. He told how he had gone before the city council when seeking a grant for his company, and had said to the council that it was foolish for the city to give away such franchises. He had urged that the public should own the street railways and operate them, just as the water-works were operated, but if the city insisted on being foolish, he hoped it would be foolish to him. As a business man he had made money out of the city's stupidity. Now he intended to see to it that nobody got what he himself had gotten, without paying for it. Under municipal ownership the city could carry passengers for three cents, if the water was squeezed out of the capital stock. Much of this water, he admitted, had been put into the companies by himself.

It was all very simple, very winning. But I could see why my friends distrusted him. Was he as candid and honest as he seemed, or was he using his frankness merely as a political blind? I was at sea. Everybody said that the city needed a business man's administration, and Mr. Johnson was certainly an eminent business man. But he was not going at it the way I felt he should. He did not seem to be a reformer. He was not indignant enough. He said nothing about waste and extravagance; about bad men; about politicians; about the spoils system. He made no personal attacks on any one. He seemed not to have a high opinion of the kind of men on whom I counted to save democracy. He held a cigar in his hand while he spoke and went away with a crowd of riotous politicians. He was not at all like my picture of the business man who was to redeem politics. . . .

The principal issue in my mind, too, was corruption. The old gang should be cleaned out, a new kind of men put in. The kind of men I had in mind were business men, trained, university men. They were my friends. The others, the bad ones, lived principally down under the hill. They were immigrants. The Thirteenth Ward was the worst; it was controlled by a Polish immigrant named Harry Bernstein. He delivered, to a man, the number of votes he promised to

deliver, to whoever would purchase them. He was the city
scandal. It was Bernsteinism that ruled the city and Bernsteinism that must be wiped out. The risk of being dirtied by
politics had to be taken; the sacrifice involved in running for
office had to be made. And I was proud to have been selected
by my friends, by the good people of my district, to make the
sacrifice.

But the riddle of Tom Johnson remained. When I could
spare time from my own campaigning, I went to his meetings.
He would go to a Republican meeting and ask permission to
talk from the same platform with the Republican candidate
for mayor. When permission was denied him, the crowd
followed him out into the street, almost emptying the hall.
One night he talked about poverty; about how to be rid of it.
He said that society should be changed not by getting good
men into office, but by making it possible for all men to be
good. He said that most men would be reasonably good if they
had a chance. We had evil in the world because people were
poor. The trouble was not with people, it was with poverty.
Poverty was the cause of vice and crime. It was social
conditions that were bad rather than people. These conditions
could be changed only through politics.

This bothered me, as did most of his speeches. Surely some
people were good, while others were bad. My classifications
were simple. Roughly, the members of the University Club and
the Chamber of Commerce were good; McKisson, Bernstein,
and the politician were bad. The bad were commonly in
power; they held offices and controlled elections. They did
not do their work well and were paid very much more than
they should receive. At the primaries they elected their own
kind of office. The way to change this vicious circle, I thought,
was to get the good people to form committees in each ward
as had been done in my own. If these committees nominated
men who would go out and fight the politicians, if we gave
enough thought to politics—as we were under a moral
obligation to do—we should drive out the spoilsmen. It was all

quite clear to me and very simple. It was the choice between
the good and the bad.

But here was a man who said that bad people were not bad;
they were merely poor and had to fight for a living. They got
an easier living out of politics than they did working twelve
hours a day in the steel-mills. So they went into politics. And
being in the majority, they won out.

I resented what Mr. Johnson said, resented too the issues he
ignored. He made my work in the Municipal Association seem
false; made it seem as if we were trying to patch up something
that ought not to be patched, that ought to be done away with
entirely. I think there was a time when I might have turned
against him. He was an enemy of my opinions, of my
education, of my superior position. It hurt my ego, my
self-respect, to be told that I was really not much better than
the politician and that my class was not as important as I
thought it was.

But I continued to go to his meetings while I listened to the
criticisms of my friends who branded him as insincere. I could
not understand why a man should make so much money out
of business and then admit that the way he made it was wrong;
why a rich man should advocate the things that he advocated,
especially as what he proposed would take money away from
his old friends. Still, much of what he said seemed true to me.
Perhaps his personality was winning me; perhaps somewhere in
the back of my mind there was approval of his ideas. I
fluttered about him mentally, accepting, withdrawing, irresist-
ibly attracted. . . .

"Why don't you cut loose," I asked, "from Charlie Salen
and the other politicians whom the people distrust? If you do
that, you will make an appeal to all the people I know. You
are a business man and we all want a business man's
administration. Then you could get the young men of the east
end, the business men, the educated classes, to support you."

"No," he replied, "they will never support me. They can't
support me. There is nothing I could say and nothing I could

do that would make it possible for the 'good people,' as you term them, to support me. This fight cuts too deep. It touches too many interests, banks, business, preachers, doctors, lawyers, clubs, newspapers. They have to be on one side. And it isn't my side. They will be against me. The only people who can be for me are the poor people and the politicians who will have to follow the poor people when they get started."

I had still a moment of hesitation. I did not see clearly enough what he wanted to do. I had never thought of ending poverty through politics. We should always have poverty. I did not believe in working with spoilsmen. I saw that Tom Johnson was fighting his friends, men of his own class, that he took pleasure in the championship of common people. The people whom I trusted he found untrustworthy. . . .

Tom Johnson was elected mayor on the issue of municipal ownership and a three-cent fare on the street-railways. Along with a number of other men indorsed by the Municipal Association, I was returned to the council, which had enough independent members to be organized on a non-partisan basis. The beginning of the political renaissance had come. Spoilsmen, bosses, grafters would be driven out. Cleveland was to be America's pace-maker.

Mr. Johnson brought to the mayoralty extraordinary business talent and technical ability. He knew mathematics, electricity and power problems. He had been a shrewd monopolist and he knew every foot of the various street-car lines in the city. He had fought many legal battles around the obstacles placed in the laws of the State to shield the companies already in the field. Elected by a large majority, he would put his programme through, it seemed, with ease.

He did a characteristic thing by taking the oath of office as soon as the election returns were officially announced. Mayor Farley, he had discovered, was about to sign an ordinance granting the valuable lake-front property, which had been the subject of twelve years' litigation, to the railroads. To forestall this action Mr. Johnson walked into the mayor's office, and announced that he had been sworn in. In this way he entered dramatically on his ten years' administration. . . .

Not long afterward I introduced for Mayor Johnson an ordinance providing for a three-cent fare on the street-railways. This involved bringing in another company and affected the interests of Senator Hanna, of the banks, of many of our clients and the men with whom I was associated. I was conscious of increasing social alienation. At the club I was made to feel uncomfortable. Most of the people I knew were opposed to everything I did. And I began to question my classification of people, which Mr. Johnson had questioned for me in his campaign speeches. Good people, my friends, were unconcerned over bribery; they were not outraged by it when it was done by people they knew. They would not stand by criminal proceedings instituted against bribe-givers. Why, I wondered, this palsy benumbing good people? When the way was pointed out, how could they fail to rise and save the city?

Subsequent experience on the city council increased these doubts. I was interested in playgrounds for children, in public baths and dance-halls, in the opening up of parks and providing recreation for the poor. Here, I thought, is something my friends will surely rally to. Here is a way to beat the saloon, to stop crime at the source, far more efficiently than by raids or regulation. I introduced legislation for these things, showed by the experience of other cities that crime had been reduced where children were taken from the streets and given a place to play, with trained instructors to help them do so.

But my friends did not rally to such measures. On the contrary, a committee of the Chamber of Commerce denounced public baths as socialistic. There was an outcry against the wider use of the parks, especially against taking down the "Keep-off-the-Grass" signs. Reform councilmen protested that these things would increase the popularity of Mayor Johnson and would add to the tax-rate. Such support as came to me, came from the old gang. In time the measures came out of the committees where they had lain for weeks and were passed with the aid of the men whom I had previously denounced. The bad men in the council rallied to the children. They knew

better than I did where the children lived and where they had
to play. On measures where there was no money moving they
voted right; while representatives from the east-end wards
often voted wrong.

In the end, through the activity of Mr. Johnson, Cleveland
acquired a city-wide system of parks, playgrounds, and public
baths. On Saturday and Sunday the whole population played
baseball in hundreds of parks laid out for that purpose.
Cleveland became a play city, and this generous provision for
play has declared dividends. Workmen like to live in Cleveland.
Workmen are followed by factory-owners. The growth for
Cleveland in the last decade is partly traceable to the policy of
making the city an attractive place in which to live.

In spite of its initial confusion and in spite of disappoint-
ments my term on the city council was one of happy activity.
I grew to love the city and the big problems it presented. I
visited other cities to study police administration, methods of
street-cleaning, the grouping of public buildings. The city
appealed to me as a social agency of great possibilities; at an
insignificant cost it could fill the lives of people with pleasure.
It could protect the poor by more intelligent use of the police
force. It could provide things at wholesale; could open
playgrounds and public baths. It could develop the lake front
into a beautiful, long esplanade. It could take over the
charities and run them as public agencies. I no longer believed
in private charity. It seemed unfair that men and women who
had given their lives to industry should have to rely upon
private benevolence when in need. I saw endless possibilities of
beauty in Cleveland.

I was conscious, as time went on, of increasing isolation.
True, it was partly of my own making, for I withdrew more
and more into myself. I shrank from old friends who dis-
approved of me. I kept away from the clubs. What was the use,
I said, of always inviting a row? It confused me that my
friends did not see things as I did; that there was not generous
approval of Tom Johnson when it became apparent that he
was giving the city a clean, businesslike administration. I could

understand the first questionings—I had had them myself—but they could not outlast a demonstration of his sincerity. But approval had not come from people I knew, from the Municipal Association, from the Chamber of Commerce, from young men who were open-minded on other things.

I was caught between two herds. I had come to like the politicians; I got on with them in the council, in ward meetings, in political conferences. They were human, generous, kindly, and for the most part did as Mr. Johnson told them to do. They were happy in his leadership; many of them turned out to be highly efficient in their jobs. But they were not my kind. With Mr. Johnson gone, they would follow any other leader. I could not be permanently identified with them anyway. And I missed friendliness, approval, a herd, that satisfied my university picture of the role I should play. . . . Mr. Johnson called his ten years' fight against privilege a war for "A City on a Hill." To the young men in the movement, and to tens of thousands of the poor who gave it their support, it was a moral crusade rarely paralleled in American politics. The struggle involved the banks, the press, the Chamber of Commerce, the clubs, and the social life of the city. It divided families and destroyed friendships. You were either for Tom Johnson or against him. If for him, you were a disturber of business, a Socialist, to some an anarchist. Had the term "Red" been in vogue, you would have been called a communist in the pay of Soviet Russia. Every other political issue and almost every topic of conversation was subordinated to the struggle.

The possibility of a free, orderly, and beautiful city became to me an absorbing passion. Here were all of the elements necessary to a great experiment in democracy. Here was a rapidly growing city with great natural advantages and with few mistakes to correct. Here was a wonderful hinterland for the building of homes, a ten-mile water-front that could be developed for lake commerce, a population that had showed itself willing to follow an ideal, and, most important of all, a great leader.

The New Deal & the Boss

This selection, taken from Lyle Dorsett's recent book,
Franklin Roosevelt and the City Bosses, *described the 1930's
political machine of Thomas J. Pendergast of Kansas City.
Pendergast inherited some political influence from his brother,
James, who first gained control of Kansas City politics; but
Thomas Pendergast's power expanded in the 1930's when he
supported Franklin Roosevelt and the national Democratic
party. In return for political support, Pendergast acquired
federal funds and additional patronage jobs to oil his political
machine and to build "his" city. Thus the federal government's emergence as a partner in the governing of the cities
during the New Deal strengthened local political machines and
catapulted local bosses into the national spotlight. Conversely,
Pendergast also discovered that national politicians could
tamper with his political power base. According to Dorsett,
Franklin Roosevelt assisted in the eventual overthrow of
Pendergast and the substitution of supposed "reform" elements. After the 1930's city bosses were forced to play
politics on a national level. The new partner in city government resided in Washington not down the street in a local
union hall or corporation headquarters.*

Thomas Joseph Pendergast, a short, round man with a bald head, sparkling dark eyes, and genuinely warm smile, met a fate similar to that of most of the city bosses who aligned themselves with Franklin D. Roosevelt. As long as he was a political asset to the president, he was showered with favors from Washington. But once it was assured that he was a political liability, Roosevelt destroyed him without blinking or flinching.

In 1933 Tom Pendergast seemed to be as firmly established in Missouri politics as the Pope was in the Roman Catholic Church. He had a dependable machine in Kansas City and rural Jackson County. The 1932 election brought victory to his hand-picked gubernatorial candidate Guy B. Park. And with Park's ascent to the governor's mansion, all the state patronage went to the machine. As a federal investigator from Washington remarked, "It is observable that through Park, Pendergast gets the state appointments. The state house is lousy with Pendergast men."

Besides the state patronage, the Kansas City boss soon had complete control of nearly all federal patronage in Missouri, until by the mid-thirties he had what was probably the best organized Democratic machine in any state of the Union with the possible exception of Hague's New Jersey organization. What is incredible is that by 1938 it suddenly began to crumble; by 1939 the boss was in federal prison; and by the time of Roosevelt's third election, the Pendergast machine was only a legend.

The meteoric rise and fall of the House of Pendergast is an interesting story which cannot be understood outside of a New Deal context. Pendergast's control of Kansas City and Jackson County was seldom challenged by the time of Roosevelt's first election, but Republicans had controlled the state house throughout the twenties. The national Democratic landslide in 1932 insured a Democrat's becoming governor. That the governor would be a Pendergast man was undisputed, inas-

Lyle Dorsett, Franklin Roosevelt and the City Bosses *(Port Washington, New York: Kenniket Press, 1977).*

much as the man from Kansas City had the largest and only dependable Democratic machine in the state. His domination of the Missouri Democrats was an established fact.

The depression no doubt made a Democratic victory inevitable in Missouri in 1932. This in itself would have given Pendergast control of the state patronage and purse strings. That Roosevelt, rather than Al Smith or someone else, became president had a marked effect on Pendergast's control of federal programs, and these programs extraordinarily enhanced his position of power in the Show-Me State.

It all began in 1931 when Pendergast went to New York and met with Governor Roosevelt, Jim Farley, and Ed Flynn. There he agreed to support them at the national convention the following summer. The result of Pendergast's early jump onto the Roosevelt-for-President bandwagon was the promise of federal patronage if the New York governor won the election. As was pointed out in chapter 1, Pendergast backed Roosevelt at the convention, and then put his machine into high gear during the autumn campaign.

Soon after the inauguration in 1933 the administration began dispersing the federal spoils. Jim Farley announced to the Missouri senator, Bennett Clark (a St. Louisian and not a member of Pendergast's organization), that a portion of patronage usually reserved for senators was going to Pendergast. Clark was furious, but Farley informed the senator that it had been promised to the Kansas City boss, who in Farley's words "was with us from the start."

With Roosevelt's blessing Farley bent over backwards to do favors for Tom Pendergast. One of the things he did was to intervene in the appointment of Missouri's state director of federal reemployment. It seems that Secretary of Labor Frances Perkins appointed a Republican from the little town of Maryville to be director. But the ink was barely dry on the secretary's selection when the appointment was withdrawn, and Pendergast's hand-picked choice, a judge from Jackson County named Harry Truman, was given the post.

Farley always did his best to help Tom Pendergast. The two

men got along extremely well, partly because they were so much alike. It is true that Farley never condoned graft or corruption, and he certainly deplored ballot box stuffing. But none of these offenses was proved to be part of Pendergast's modus operandi until 1939, so for years Farley never had to apologize for associating with the Missouri boss. Actually, the two men had much in common. Both were of Irish ancestry; they came from very humble beginnings and were dedicated individuals who had worked hard to pull themselves up by their own bootstraps. Lifelong Democrats, each believed in party discipline and loyalty. They saw the Democratic Party as the acme of democracy. Anyone was welcome to work for the party. If one worked and the party won, then he deserved a share of the spoils. To the two Irishmen this was Jacksonian Democracy in its purest form. The system was as American as apple pie; it had been around for a hundred years, and it worked. They were living proof. Both had worked hard for the party, and both were on top.

Pendergast's close relationship with James A. Farley was an important asset to the Kansas City Democratic organization. Even though Pendergast did not have the advantage of hobnobbing with the president as La Guardia did, he had the ear of one of the most powerful men in the administration. Farley's favors were extremely important to Pendergast, but equally helpful were the personal visits. Every time Farley, who was chairman of the Democratic National Committee and postmaster general of the United States, came to Kansas City, lights flashed and sirens roared. A big shot from Washington was in Kansas City — and he had come to see Big Tom.

Identification with Farley added prestige to the Pendergast machine, but probably nothing did as much to strengthen it in Kansas City as the federal work relief programs. The skyline of Kansas City is a lasting legacy of New Deal programs. Whoever approaches Kansas City by automobile or airplane is struck by a complex of skyscrapers in the heart of the business district. Among them are the city hall, the county court house, and the police station. The construction costs of these buildings, as

well as the city's beautiful and functional convention hall and
municipal auditorium (which covers a square city block), were
paid for in part by federal grants through such agencies as
PWA, CWA, and WPA. Viewed as a whole, these structures
gave Kansas City an unusually attractive, modern face lifting.
The building complex also provided the community with
facilities for conventions, athletic events, and city and county
business that were far superior to those in most cities of
comparable size in the country.

Pendergast, who owned the Ready-Mixed Concrete Company, made a small fortune from the contracts his company
won to build many of these structures. Realizing the popularity of this immense building program, he did not hesitate to
take advantage of it. In 1938, for example, just before the city
elections, the boss ran a "Progress Edition" of the *Missouri
Democrat*, a newspaper which he controlled. In this special
edition were editorials and pictures which focused on the
machine-controlled city administration and all that it had done
to bring progress to the midwestern metropolis. One section of
the paper was reserved for Ready-Mixed Concrete advertising.
Beneath a photograph of the new city hall, a structure made
possible through WPA grants, appeared the following boldface
line: "PERMANENCE— We are proud to have had a part in
the construction of so many Kansas City buildings."

Taking partial credit for construction programs and identi-
fying closely with such a prominent national figure as Farley
aided the machine in innumerable ways. A form of support
which was more tangible, and for that matter ultimately more
important to the machine, was federal patronage. CWA, which
lasted less than a full year, put 100,000 men and almost
10,000 women to work on the federal payroll in Missouri. It is
impossible to say how much of this patronage was directed by
Pendergast and his lieutenants. However, it is clear that he
controlled all of Kansas City's share of the spoils, and it was a
lion's share.

The single most important boost that the machine received
from Washington, however, was control of the WPA. After

1935, and until it was phased out with the war, there were always 80,000 to 90,000 persons on the WPA payrolls in Missouri. That Pendergast absolutely controlled this patronage and used it to strengthen his hold on the entire state is beyond question.

The director of federal work relief for Missouri was Matthew S. Murray, a Kansas Citian and close friend of Pendergast. Harry Hopkins controlled the federal work relief programs at the national level, and appointed a director for each state. Normally, the senators of each state recommended a candidate for the directorship to Hopkins, and he then gave his approval. Missouri's senators, Truman and Clark, recommended Murray only after consultation with Pendergast. Hopkins rubberstamped the recommendation.

The state director of work relief programs was a powerful person. An eminently fair director could distribute jobs and programs largely on the basis of need. But unfortunately, many state directors used the position as a political weapon. They rewarded loyal party workers with soft or high-paying jobs, channeled an inordinate amount of funds into their home counties, and even coerced rank and file employees to vote for favored candidates in primaries and general elections.

Missouri's Matthew Murray was no exception. A loyal member of the Pendergast machine, he was described by one of Boss Pendergast's lieutenants as a man who has been ". . . extra close to T.J. [Pendergast], and has proved himself LOYALTY itself to the man. Murray came here thru Willie Ross of the Ross Construction Company [of which Pendergast was part owner], off the State Highway Department. . . . He was unknown to T.J.P. Yet, he played ball, made good and soon was a schooled and close-mouthed public official." That Kansas City's political machine was given complete control of federal work relief programs is abundantly clear. Citizens in the state who were unemployed and seeking federal assistance often wrote to the governor, hoping he would help them find a position with the WPA. Governor Guy B. Park always replied to such inqiuries by saying that the person must get in touch

with Matthew S. Murray, inasmuch as he "will be in complete
charge of Federal work relief in Missouri." Even Senator Harry
S Truman bowed to the Pendergast machine before helping his
constituents find federal jobs. To a man seeking senatorial aid
in finding WPA employment, Truman replied: "If you will
send us endorsements from the Kansas City Democratic
Organization, I shall be glad to do what I can for you."

Lloyd Stark, the man who was to be endorsed by
Pendergast for governor in 1936, was told just how important
the federal work relief program was to the machine. "With
Murray in the saddle to see that it is administered . . . [you
know] just what is to be reckoned with [because] . . . we are
not fools." Stark discovered what the informant meant when
he ran for the gubernatorial nomination in 1936. Because he
had Pendergast's endorsement, all the powers of the machine
were put into action. Sworn testimony shows that WPA
employees all over the state voted for Stark, and they were
told they would lose their jobs if they refused. In the same
vein it is clear that when he ran in the general election that
same year, there were people on the federal payroll working
on his behalf once again.

The WPA became an integral part of Pendergast's statewide
organization. In virtually every county there were federal
employees who faithfully worked for the machine's candidates. The chain of command in the WPA was neatly tied into
politics and usually worked quite effectively. Most district
directors of WPA had their jobs because they already had put
in years of loyal service with the machine. Out of appreciation
for their high-paying positions, they pressured the workers in
their districts to vote as they were instructed. The amount of
pressure placed on the rank and file workers varied, depending
upon the determination and judgment of the director involved.
In many instances, employees were simply asked to vote for
the organization's ticket. More aggressive directors bought
their workers a beer and then asked them to vote the machine
line. Some bosses were militant and threatened to fire
employees who were stubborn, whereas others argued that if

Harry S Truman, Thomas J. Pendergast, James P. Aylward, James Farley, N. G. Robertson and David A. Fitzgerald at the Democratic National Convention in Philadelphia, June 1936. ACME Newspictures — UPI

the machine's candidates were not elected the WPA would be removed from Missouri. Holding loss of employment over the heads of workers was exceedingly effective. Indeed, one candidate for statewide office who was opposed by Pendergast actually wrote off hopes of carrying certain counties for precisely this reason.

In the final analysis, the New Deal strengthened the Pendergast machine. The favors from New Dealers such as Farley, the construction program in Kansas City and throughout the state, plus the tens of thousands of jobs on the federal payroll, all conspired to strengthen Pendergast's hold on Kansas City and Jackson County and to expand his influence all over Missouri. Machine candidates carried every election in Kansas City during the 1930's, and by higher margins each time. Likewise, Big Tom's candidates in statewide elections were almost always nominated and without exception elected until 1938.

In return for all the help which he received from the Roosevelt administration, the intense, chain-smoking boss of Kansas City delivered the votes for Roosevelt. The Missouri delegation went to the national convention in 1936 100 percent behind the president. And when election time rolled around, everyone labored diligently for the reelection of Roosevelt. Moreover, the machine delivered an overwhelming majority to the incumbent, just as it had promised.

After the election of 1936 Thomas Pendergast seemed invulnerable. His people were in every major elective and appointive office in Kansas City, Jackson County, and the state of Missouri. In addition, he was in complete control of federal work relief programs in the state. To most observers the name "Pendergast" would continue to be synonymous with power in Missouri politics because Roosevelt had been reelected, and the boss's candidate Lloyd C. Stark was ready to move into the governor's mansion.

Few Missourians would have believed in November 1936 that the fall of Pendergast was imminent—that he would be in the federal penitentiary and the machine would be a shambles in less than thirty-six months. Incredible as it may seem, it happened; and Franklin Roosevelt played no small role in the drama.

The fall of the Pendergast machine really commenced when Lloyd Stark was elected governor. Stark was a rural Missourian who had made a fortune from apples. He was the owner of Stark Brothers Nurseries, which produced the nationally famous "Stark's Delicious Apples." He was an extremely ambitious politician, but was blocked from seeking a second term in 1940 because Missouri law prohibited a governor from succeeding himself. To continue in public life in a position equal to or higher than the one he held, the apple grower had to consider the senatorial nomination in 1940. But Harry Truman would only complete his freshman term in 1940 and certainly would seek reelection with the blessings of the powerful Pendergast machine.

Stark's strategy gradually became clear. What he was about to do, and in alliance with President Roosevelt, was unbelievable to Tom Pendergast. It is true that the Kansas City boss had voted a few ghosts in his day. And it is true that he violated the public trust by lining his own pocket. However, Pendergast really did not see anything terribly wrong in that. He had, after all, spent thousands of dollars out of his own pocket on the poor people in Kansas City. Nobody who sought the boss's help was ever turned away.

Furthermore, Pendergast played politics by an inflexible code — you kept your word. If you made a promise for support, you delivered after election day. If you accepted support, you divided the spoils among your allies once the victory was won. The idea of knifing a supporter in the back was totally foreign to the rules of the political game as Pendergast played it. It was unheard of to bite the hand that fed you. Consequently, Pendergast was unprepared for the attacks launched against him by Stark and Roosevelt. The Kansas City boss might have protected himself beforehand, but he simply never believed that the man he elevated to the state capital would try to destroy him, or that the president he stuck his neck out for as early as 1931 would provide the weapon.

A number of events conspired which gave Stark an opportunity for political advancement. First of all, the federal district attorney in Kansas City, Maurice Milligan, conducted an investigation of the 1936 election. He discovered large-scale vote fraud and ultimately convicted 259 of 278 defendants. These cases dragged through the federal court for two years, all the time reminding the public of a seamy side of the Pendergast machine.

As the convictions for vote fraud piled up, many citizens grew critical of the machine and some of its other illegal activities. Governor Stark's office was inundated during those months with letters from irate citizens who demanded that he clean up the police department in Kansas City, which was protecting gambling, prostitution, and after-hours drinking establishments.

At some point Stark envisioned a plan to vault himself into the United States Senate in 1940. If he could shroud himself in the garb of a reformer, expose large-scale graft in the Pendergast machine, and smear Truman through guilt by association (Pendergast hand-picked Truman for the Senate in 1934), there would be no way to block his march to Washington.

Stark embarked upon a campaign where he did all he could to attract attention to himself as a reformer and enemy of Boss Pendergast. First he reduced Kansas City's fair share of state patronage, and then he began firing all state employees who had been recommended by Pendergast in the first months of the administration. After that he launched an all-out campaign to halt the gambling and illegal liquor traffic in Missouri's western metropolis.

Pendergast, embittered and hurt by these attacks from the man he put into the governor's chair not long before, publicly condemned Stark as an "ingrate." But Stark, undaunted, had just started his fight. Obviously convinced he could destroy the big boss, his next move was for the jugular. In early 1938 the governor and Federal District Attorney Milligan went to the nation's capital. Feeling confident that Pendergast somewhere along the line had misappropriated funds, they consulted the secretary of the treasury and urged a thorough investigation of the boss. Ultimately, Stark and Milligan were responsible for getting T-men and the FBI to sift through every scrap of paper in Kansas City that related to Thomas Joseph Pendergast.

While this investigation was underway, the governor challenged the boss in the primary election in August 1938. Each man put a candidate in the primary for the state supreme court, and each man used every tool at his disposal to win. The stakes were high. The entire state, as well as the powers in Washington, were watching to see if the apple grower from rural Missouri could topple the big Irishman's urban-based

machine. Pendergast put his forces into motion. The state
employees he could no longer touch, but those holding WPA
jobs were pressured to the limit. Stark, on the other hand, had
the state's job holders under his thumb. They were forced to
contribute money to the campaign fund, sport bumper stickers
on their cars, and personally escort voters to the polls.

After an unusually bitter campaign Stark's candidate won
by a narrow margin. The loss was much more to Pendergast
than the supreme court slot on the Democratic ticket.
Franklin D. Roosevelt had been watching the race through his
narrow political lenses. He concluded that Pendergast was dead
in Missouri, and that Stark was the Democrat to court. Almost
as soon as the votes were tallied, the president took up with
the "reform" governor.

Farley did all that he could for Pendergast, but to no avail.
Early that year Maurice Milligan's term as federal district
attorney expired, and he was to be considered for reappoint-
ment. Senator Truman urged another appointment be made,
and Farley seconded the motion. The president, however, was
"cold toward any change in that office," according to Farley.

The election scandal of 1936 had made Roosevelt less than
enthusiastic about Pendergast; hence his refusal to dump
Milligan. But after Stark won the 1938 primary, Roosevelt
grew militantly anti-Pendergast. The president deliberately
ignored the wishes of the Kansas City boss on every bit of
federal patronage. Realizing full well that Truman was an
active member of the machine, Roosevelt refused to approve
traditionally senatorial federal appointments which were
recommended by Truman, without first checking with Governor Stark. This infuriated Farley, who urged Roosevelt to keep
in mind that a governor should not be consulted on federal
appointments. But Roosevelt was convinced that the Missouri
Democrats would be under Stark's control by 1940, and he
wanted to be in favor with the power elite.

As will be emphasized when Roosevelt's relationship with
Hague and Kelly is compared to that with Pendergast, he did
not dump the Kansas City boss because of moral indignation.

Corruption he could tolerate as long as the parties involved were men of power and useful to him. By 1938 Roosevelt shunned Pendergast not because he was morally outraged, but because he believed Pendergast had become a loser.

By spring 1939 the federal investigation had paid rich dividend to Stark and Milligan. Pendergast was charged with a ten-year period of income tax evasion. The tired, sad-eyed boss pleaded guilty. Having recently suffered a severe heart attack and undergone three abdominal operations, he was not up to fighting this battle—one which he was certain to lose anyway.

Milligan, who prosecuted Pendergast, and Stark, who had instigated the drive against the boss, both were elated when the judge sentenced him to fifteen months in federal prison and five years probation thereafter. Pendergast started serving his sentence in Fort Leavenworth, Kansas, at about the same time Stark launched his campaign to unseat Harry Truman from the United States Senate.

Truman's victory over the two "reformers" must have warmed the heart of Tom Pendergast. To be sure, there was little else to brighten those last years of his life. When he returned from prison in 1940, he brought one last wish. According to his friends, he hoped that the man he had agreed to support for the presidential nomination back in 1931 would bestow him one favor before he died. Pendergast implored Roosevelt to grant him a pardon so that he would have the rights of American citizenship once again before his death.

Wrapped in a cloak of self-righteousness, the Hyde Park aristocrat snubbed the dying Kansas City boss. Big Tom died in January 1945—his one last wish never granted. If he could have held on a few more weeks, he most certainly would have received that presidential pardon. Truman, who was elected vice president in 1944, was less than eighty days away from the presidency. That Truman would have pardoned the man who gave him his start in politics there can be little doubt. Only Vice President Truman had the courage to go to Kansas City for Pendergast's funeral. After all, said the man from Independence, "he was my friend."

Just before he died, the big Irishman told a reporter from a Missouri newspaper, "I've never broken my word to any living human being I gave it to." Certainly the president of the United States, who had only a few months to live himself, could never have said the same thing honestly.

Richard J. Daley, Modern Boss

*On April 20, 1955, Richard J. Daley became mayor of the
nation's second largest city. Since that time his rule over the
Chicago Democratic party and Chicago politics persisted
virtually without opposition until his death in 1976. None of
the twentieth-century city bosses – Curley of Boston,
Lawrence of Pittsburgh, or Kelly of Chicago – held power
longer than Richard Daley. His critics contended that he was
the last of the big city bosses, an anachronism. They charged
him with running roughshod over the democratic process by
catering to the special interests of wealthy minorities. According to Daley's critics, his greatest fault was his neglect of the
need of the city's poor and black citizens.*

*Daley's supporters, however, claimed that Chicago was the
most efficiently run city in the nation. "In Chicago," one
Daley supporter remarked, "things get done." As evidence
they pointed to projects such as the Dan Ryan, Adlai
Stevenson, and JFK expressways, the new Chicago Circle
campus of the University of Illinois, O'Hare International
Airport, and the new civic center with its fifty-foot Picasso
sculpture.*

In the following essay David Halberstam, journalist and

*author of a recent best-selling book dealing with the Kennedy
administration, discusses the personality and power of Richard
Daley and the Chicago Democratic machine. Halberstam's
essay urges one to consider the similarities and differences
between Daley and city bosses of the past.*

In the political year 1968, Richard J. Daley surveyed the
city of Chicago and was master of it. He exercised power as
probably no man outside of Washington exercised it, and he
was by most norms of the American ethic, particularly his
own, a towering success. The poor of his city were afraid of
him and the powerful of the nation deferred to him.

It was his city to an extraordinary degree, and now his
party was coming to his city to choose a President. The more
contested the nomination would be, the more the poor blacks
and the long-haired white kids worked in the primaries to
offset the Democratic party establishment, why, yes, the more
powerful Richard J. Daley would be in August; and he was
aware of this, aware that in his own way he could dominate
the convention, and though there might be other men more
popular, more handsome, more beloved, the final decisions
would be made by Mayor Daley. (Early in the year, when
Robert Kennedy made his entrance into the race and a reporter asked a Daley man which hotel in Chicago Kennedy
would be taking over, the Daley man answered, with the sense
of certainty that only the very powerful have, "Bobby Kennedy isn't taking over anything in *this* city.") He would walk
into the convention erect and powerful (particularly if his city
were not in flames), and his words would be sought by the
nation's foremost reporters, though surely they would be
platitudinous, for he specialized in platitudes. He had learned
long ago that if possible you spoke platitudes or you spoke not
at all.

Everywhere there would be reminders to the guests that

they were in Dick Daley's Chicago. In a profession where
municipal officials keeled over like flies after one or two
terms, especially if they were effective, thrown out by angry
undertaxed constituents who felt themselves overtaxed, who
hated the parking and the air and their neighbors, Richard J.
Daley reigned supreme, King Richard as he was called in
Chicago.

Four times he was elected, the fourth by his largest majority, 74 percent. His years of success had virtually left Chicago
without an electoral process, *that* was his achievement; in a
city where few new buildings had been started before him, the
sky was pierced again and again by new skyscrapers, each
bigger and more gleaming than the last, and ever-grateful rich
and aristocratic businessmen taught from the cradle to shun
the Democratic party — that party of the machine and the
Irish — competed to enlist in Republicans for Daley, vowed to
give bigger contributions, while the most famous political
scientists of Chicago, hawks and doves, liberals and conserva-
tives, joined Professors for Daley. Municipal experts, techno-
crats with their measuring sticks, were in general agreement
that Daley was the most successful Mayor in America — good
cost accounting, good police department, good fire department, good social-economic programs. He was a politician with
a smooth-functioning political machine in an age when machines were not supposed to function. (When one reporter for
a local paper saw him at a meeting, a man who knew a
machine when he saw one, Daley would say simply, "Organization, not machine. Get that. Organization, not machine.")

His city vibrated with those traditional American ingredi-
ents, vitality, energy, ambition, business drive, and racial failure, and it was because of these that Daley's role in history
seemed curiously in doubt, for all his great achievements. In
America now, when everything else failed, when the family
failed and the churches failed and the system failed, the good
Mayor would get the blame, not the Mayors of Natchez,
Mississippi, or Clarksdale, Mississippi, or of thousands of other
towns which had exported so many illiterate young Negroes

Mayor Richard Daley. Summer 1972. Photo courtesy Chicago Historical Society.

North in the last fifteen years: the blame would be on the
Mayor of the city which received them and which, as they had
been failed once before, failed them again.

For Richard Daley presided over a city which had burned
once and had a special tinderbox quality. It contained angry
backlashing whites, some of the greatest backlashers in America who had finally managed to buy little homes in Chicago
and paid their taxes there, and angry, frustrated, forelashing
blacks. It was a city which contained one great Negro ghetto
and another area which was not even a ghetto; it was a jungle,
the kids alley-tough, totally outside the system, larger kids
shaking down the smaller ones, youth gangs with organizational charts like the Army. Other cities were this bad, and
some were worse, and in many of the older ways Richard J.
Daley had done more for the Negro, to use that term, than
many other Mayors. But there was also a suspicion that part of
the problem was Daley, that his machine had been too smart
for itself, and that finally Daley was perhaps not equipped to
understand the complexity and the intense pressures of new
times. Even his image seemed wrong, a point about which his
staff was particularly sensitive. One of Daley's press people
could point to a photograph of John Lindsay on the cover of
Life and gloat over the headline, "Small acts and big plans,"
saying, "We could kill Lindsay with that. We could run against
him and destroy him. Lindsay? What's he ever done? What
programs has he got? Lindsay's people come out here for
lessons in government."

It was not just Daley, it was America, with all the chickens,
one hundred years or more in flight, coming home to roost.
"Daley may well personify the Achilles' heel of America," one
Negro critic said. "He's taken many positions not because he's
outside the mainstream of America, but precisely because he's
in it, which doesn't say a hell of a lot for either Daley or
America."

For in a sense Chicago seemed to be the real capital of
America, a strong, tough, vital city where the American business ethic worked, a city largely without reform influence

("We think of reform as being an effete Easterner idea," said
one transplanted New Yorker). Nelson Algren, Chicago's
uncrowned poet laureate, could write in his "Ode to Lower
Finksville":

> City of the big gray-flanneled shoulders
> Fierce as a dog with tongue lapping for action
> How come you spend all that great ferocity
> On the windpipes of The Down, The Out and
>   and The Defenseless
> And keep all that great lapping for overfed
>   real-estate hogs?

So Daley and Chicago seemed to symbolize America; he was
ours, for better and for worse, in sickness and in health.

Other Choices, Other Times

Richard J. Daley is the product of the politics of another
time. "I think one of the real problems he has with Negroes is
understanding that the Irish are no longer the out-ethnic
group," one Negro says. He would be doomed in the cosmetol-
ogy of today's politics: those jowls, that heavy-set look. He
doesn't look like a modern municipal leader, a cost-accounting
specialist; he looks, yes, exactly like a big city boss, right out
of the smoke-filled room. "Daley will never really get a fair
judging on his abilities as a mayor because of the way he
looks," an admiring Chicago political scientist says. "He's
much better than people think."

When he was first elected he spoke badly — "dese" and
"dems" — but he has worked hard and now has very considerable control over most of his political appearances; there has
also been a sharp decline in his malapropisms, though some
Chicago reporters still collect them. Two of the best are *we
will reach greater and greater platitudes of achievement,* and
*they have vilified me, they have crucified me, yes they have
even criticized me.* He is not good on the tube, but it is a
mistake to underestimate his power and charm in person. "He
exudes" one fellow Irishman says "the confidence and power
of a man who has achieved everything he set out to do and

then a little more, but he also has the black moods of an
Irishman and if you catch him in one of those it can be pretty
frightening."

He dominates Chicago and he knows it, and this adds to his
confidence. "People are always coming to me and telling me
that they're going down to see the Mayor and tell him off,"
one Negro remarks, and off they go, and of course he charms
them completely and they come back and I ask, 'Well, brother,
how did it go?' and they tell me, 'Why, the Mayor's a fine man
and we *know*' — get that, we know — 'he's going to do the
right thing.' " But clever, resounding speech is not his forte,
and he has learned that the less you say now, the less you have
to regret later, and indeed the problem may go away by then.
He has made a political virtue out of being inarticulate. He has
been satisfied with being Mayor, has consolidated his base
there, has never let his ambition run away with him; this is
part of the explanation for his power. He has sat there with a
power base, slowly adding to it, incorporating new men as
they rose, always looking for winners. Above all else Richard
Daley loves power and winners. An aide of John Kennedy's
remembers arriving in Chicago in 1960 for the first television
debate and Kennedy asking again and again, "Where's Daley,
where's Daley," with no Daley to be found. "But after the
debate," the aide recalls, "the first person to break through
into the studio, with his flunkies around him like a flying
wedge, was Daley. He knew he had a winner."

He was a poor Irish boy, born in a time when the Irish felt
themselves despised in Protestant America. One reason,
according to friends, that he was so close to Joseph Kennedy
was that they both shared the same boyhood scars. Daley's
father was a sheet-metal worker and an early union activist,
blacklisted at several plants. There were few avenues open to
an ambitious young Irish boy in those days and one of them
was politics; though he is widely admired by all of Chicago's
business giants today for his financial acumen, it is a fact of
life, of which both are sharply aware, that he could not have
made it in their world at that time.

More than most great men of power in America he is what he was. He lives in the same neighborhood where he was born, in the same house in which he has lived all his married life. He attends early Mass every day and observes the same basic tenets of the Catholic faith that he has based his life upon. His friends are the same small cluster of men, very much like himself, whom he has always known. His success has thrown him into the orbit of newer and more important men, but he has never crossed the line between association and friendship. His personal views remain rigid and he expects others to have the same; one reporter remembers a Daley son coming back from college recently with an unduly long haircut; Daley simply nodded at Matt Danaher, one of his deputies, and the boy was taken out for a trimming.

He is now acknowledged master of the Democratic party machinery which gave him his start. The machine ethic was based upon hard work and loyalty; you worked your way up level by level. But loyalty rather than brilliance or social conscience or originality was the determining characteristic. It was and is a profession which abounded in limited men and hacks, of small men trying to throw around the power of bigger men, which often they only sniff at. Daley, apprenticing in a world of hacks, was and is no hack. He is an intelligent, strong-willed man, enormously hard-working. He set out within the party organization and mastered it, working his way up from precinct captain to committeeman to state legislator, a good one, easily distinguished from most of the men in Springfield, in his room every night studying the legislation. He was a young man who played by the rules of the game. He never frightened anyone, never looked too ambitious, accumulating political due bills all the time. He also mastered the art of finance as few active politicians in America have, eventually becoming director of revenue for Governor Adlai Stevenson. . . .

Chicago's Brand of Toughness
Chicago is rougher than other cities. Even today its more

sophisticated citizens take a quiet pleasure in talking about not only its past sins but its present vices and the current power of the crime Syndicate. The city's rough edge is often a little hard for Easterners to understand. A few years ago a Negro alderman named Ben Lewis was shot down in cold blood. A correspondent for an Eastern magazine was immediately cabled by his New York office for a piece which would include, among other things, the outraged reaction of the good people of Chicago. There was no outrage at all, he cabled back. "The feeling is that if he's an alderman, he's a crook, and if he's a crook then that's their business."

The kind of money which focuses on reform politics in New York simply does not exist in Chicago and the machine has traditionally understood the reformers better than the reformers have understood the machine. Reformers have one district locally from which their candidates harass the machine (this year one of the ablest reformers, Abner Mikva, is running for Congress with the support of the machine, a truce not uncommon in Chicago politics), and indeed are occasionally placed on the ticket statewide to broaden its base and serve as a safety valve to keep reformers from going after the machine, though, as far as the machine is concerned, a U.S. Senate seat, and the Governorship are minor offices. The races for state's attorney and state assessor (who can investigate and harass the machine) are much more important.

Thus in 1948, the year that Stevenson was running for Governor and Paul Douglas for the Senate, a golden year, a liberal happened to run into Colonel Jacob Arvey, then boss of the machine. "How's the election going?" the reformer asked. "Fine, fine, couldn't be better," Arvey answered. "The polls show Boyle [state's attorney] way way ahead."

The Chicago machine had prospered under the New Deal, prospered to the point of venality, until it made Chicago probably the most corrupt city in the country. Everything could be bought or sold. The police force was largely concerned with street-corner traffic courts and the downtown center of the city was dying fast. So a reform movement was started behind Martin Kennelly, a clean and handsome businessman. He ran in 1951 as a reform candidate and won. The reformers were delighted; so were the Syndicate and the machine. It became easier to steal than before; underneath the surface honesty almost everything went wrong. Kennelly was totally naive about a very tough city. To this day, a lot of Daley critics, knowing his faults and failings, think of John Lindsay and see Martin Kennelly.

The local Chicago establishment was so disturbed about the Kennelly years that an informal meeting was held to decide what to do about the Mayor. The first thing, they decided, was to destroy the myth that they themselves had created of the Good Reform Mayor. So they decided to approach a nationally known magazine writer and have him come in to expose Kennelly. Tom Stokes was selected and a leading lawyer was duly sent to visit him. Stokes proceeded to give him a lecture on why a nice businessman with high morals and fine ideals could never govern a city as tough as Chicago; he could never understand the balance between what the city required and what the politicians and crooks would permit. Chicago needed, Stokes said, a tough professional politician who understood the underside of Chicago life and how to control it.

His Secret Clout

Enter Richard J. Daley. When he decided to run for Mayor he already wore an important political hat, clerk of Cook County, which was like being Secretary of State for the machine; it allowed him to dispense much of the machine's patronage. Before making the race he reportedly promised Colonel Arvey that he would give up the organizational job (which he didn't and it became the secret of his success). The primary was particularly bitter and it was repeatedly charged that electing Daley would be like throwing the rascals back in.

"I would not unleash the forces of evil," he countered. "It's a lie. I will follow the training my good Irish mother gave me — and Dad. If I am elected, I will embrace mercy, love, charity, and walk humbly with my God."

Pen and ink drawing by Carrie Orr. Photo courtesy Chicago Historical Society.

The machine was split (in the same ward one precinct went for Kennelly 485 to 7, while another precinct went for Daley 400 to 10). A number of reformers such as Stevenson came out for Daley, and with the help of Bill Dawson, Lord of the Negro wards, Daley won. In the general election he was opposed by Robert Merriam, an attractive Republican candidate who gave him a hard race. It was a hard fought campaign, the question being, who's going to control Chicago, State Street or the Neighborhoods (the rich or the poor)? Daley won again, decided to be both Mayor and organization chairman, thus to

a degree breaking with Arvey. Most of his success has stemmed
from that decision; it is an extraordinary achievement to hold
both jobs with so little opposition for so long. (He was aided
in the beginning by other pols, who underestimated him and
felt he would be relatively easy to control.)

Daley's municipal ambition is backed up, to use the Chicago expression, with political clout. When he wants something done, it gets done. He knows every miniscule aspect of
the city, both municipally and politically, knows the balance
and has the political power to handle the people who don't
measure up. As one Daley aide says, "I don't know how many
times the Mayor told Bob Wagner there in New York to do the
same thing, to go one way or another, either to be a reformer
or to be like him, but to make a choice. But your city is
different in New York — your people all have more illusions
about yourselves."

From the time he took over almost thirteen years ago,
Daley has steadily increased his power; where new power
outside his sphere has risen up he has moved quickly and ably
to incorporate it, to make it his. Where problems have arisen
he has quickly appointed committees, often filled with former
business foes, and then subtly moved the committees over to
his own position. When there has been opposition, he has
moved to embrace it (carrying always the threat of his real
power if it didn't come along), to make it part of his consensus. Typically, several years ago the Republicans were pre-
pared to run an excellent group of lawyers as judges. Daley
went to them and said that if they ran as Republicans he
would move Heaven and earth to beat them; if they ran as
Democrats he would guarantee there would be no opposition.
Most ran as Democrats.

As his power increased, so did his ability to accommodate
people, and his ability to tell them to get on the team or be
frozen out. Though Daley was strongly opposed by State
Street in his first race, he has since practically destroyed the
Republican party as a force within the city. He has given the
business leaders what they want, a new downtown area, an

expressway, a decent police force, confidence in the city's economic future (and if the school system is deteriorating, their children can always go to private or suburban schools). In return he has had his projects carried out with their support, and has gotten their political backing and campaign funds. The result of this is that it has been very difficult for a serious Republican candidate to make a challenge. It takes an estimated $1.5 million to run for Mayor of Chicago and any candidate would have a hard time raising $200,000 to run against Daley.

The Democratic primary is the decisive election within the city, much more so than in New York, and within the primary, all other things being equal, the machine is the dominant force. For it still functions well. Each ward committeeman has about 500 jobs (the eleventh ward, Daley's own in the Bridgeport neighborhood, has at least twice as many), and that means that each committeeman has a base in his own area of 500 families or more from which to operate. In general, the apparatus controls about 35,000 jobs and is considered to be worth about 100,000 votes in an election. Daley is very good about seeing that every committeeman gets his fair share of patronage, but it all comes down from the Mayor; he watches the organization to see who can still cut it and who can't. Through this system there is intense local control; if one block doesn't come through, everyone from top to bottom will know whose fault it is. The people just below Daley, the key committeeman, make their money selling insurance and real estate in their fiefs. But Daley has never been touched by scandal and probably never will be. The idea that he might be interested in money instead of sheer power would shock most Chicagoans. "It is Daley's greatest success that he has managed to convince the public that he is totally honest while at the same time conveying to the pols that he will permit clean graft so long as it is not abused and does not embarrass him," one newspaperman says. But even when there are abuses, he tries to take care of the offender; it is part of the ethic of loyalty. When he was first elected Daley had to clean out the Loop,

which had become the center of crime. He carefully took all
the hoods and semi-hoods who made their living there and put
them in the Sanitation Department. About six years later the
Sanitation Department began to go rotten and they had to be
transferred again.

He has managed to keep the machine viable, to bring cost
accounting to the city government, to keep up with many
reforms in the New Deal tradition, and in the words of one
political scientist, "to make the machine a limited instrument
for social progress." He has bound together this unnatural
consensus at a particularly difficult time, and part of the
reason comes from the consensus itself; each member of it is
aware of the others and of the counterpressure on the Mayor.
This acts as a restraint; they will not push too far for fear of
rocking the boat. Part of the reason, too, is that Daley simply
works harder than his opponents. He is at early Mass when his
enemies are still sleeping, and he is still working on city
problems at night when they've all gone to bed or are out
drinking. He pays enormous attention to detail; he goes over
every job application, to a ridiculously low level. Finally he
knows more about the petty details of Chicago than almost
any of his critics. They, as Dr. Martin Luther King did,
criticize the broad outlines of life in Chicago; he comes in
armed with details of its daily life, what he is doing and what
he would like to do but can't. "The Mayor could go on
television tomorrow night and wave a wand to end discrimina-
tion but the next day life would be the same," says an aide.

He tries to control dissent in Chicago as much as he can,
and outspoken critics from some papers and radio stations
have occasionally left Chicago allegedly because of City Hall
pressure; even in City Hall, when meetings are about to be
called, there is what is known as the Ruly Crowd, made up of
faithful followers ready to sit in at any meeting to keep out a
potential Unruly Crowd. He avoids the press except on his
own terms; reporters are avoided, though publishers are not;
by Daley's maxim publishers have power and reporters do not.
Besieged by magazine writers in the spring of this year he

consented to see most of them. He was very gracious to me, sounding a little like Martin Luther King talking about race; yet I had the sense of being a mosquito bite, which once scratched would never itch again.

There was a sense that Daley was an American genius of sorts, a pragmatic man with a sense of man's corruptibility. He was successful where social reformers might have failed. He embodied many of the qualities which distinguish Chicago; he was as tough, as shrewd, ambitious, and sentimental as that city. When the Negroes, in their anger, burned Chicago, his city, his sentimental love for the place was almost childlike. He despaired; how could they do that to his city, how could they do that to him after all he had done for them? Why didn't the Negroes come forth now and show to the world how much they loved Chicago?

But Richard Daley knew more than most men where power existed, and it did not exist among the black citizens of the city. Part of this was his fault, but it was very late in the game. Now sixty-six, in what is almost surely his last term as Mayor, concerned more than anything else with his place in history, he presided over a city seething with racial problems, of steadily intensifying polarization, of a school system which was often useless; and many of the black people of the city saw him more than anyone else in the city, or the country, as the symbol of what was wrong with America. (A young Negro playwright named Ronald Fair could write a bitter play, *The Emperor's Parade*, about an Irish mayor who brings over an imported Irish leprechaun for his greatest day, the St. Patrick's Day parade, and goes berserk when it is ruined by black civil-rights marchers.) It was one of the ironies of Daley's rule of Chicago that because he had succeeded so much in other areas his failures on race relations seemed so marked. Unlike other mayors, one sensed that he had the power to do something.

Machine Politics, Chicago Style

Recent interpretations of the nineteenth-century political machine indicate that the boss received his support from three sources. Immigrants consistently voted the party line in exchange for jobs, food, and money. Big business supported the boss with political donations and illegal kickbacks. In return, the boss cut through red tape to assist business in securing franchises to operate a street railway or provide the city with water. The boss also minimized competition by granting contracts to certain favored corporations. Finally, the machine often received support from illegal businesses such as vice and the rackets. The boss frequently enabled organized crime to operate with a minimum of legal interference. In return organized crime contributed political funds and tacitly agreed to "police its own house." Under this arrangement crime flourished underground, providing services demanded by some citizens — gambling, prostitution, drugs — without arousing the moral indignation of the voters.

In the following reading Mike Royko, a Chicago newspaperman and author of a best-selling book on Mayor Daley, demonstrates how Daley's machine helped and depended on the poor, organized crime, and big business.

The Hawk and Sam, as precinct captains, are basic parts of the Machine. There are some thirty-five hundred precincts in Chicago, and every one of them has a Democratic captain and most captains have assistant captains. They all have, or can have, jobs in government. The better the captain, the better the job. Many make upwards of fifteen thousand dollars a year as supervisors, inspectors, or minor department heads.

They aren't the lowest ranking members of the Machine. Below them are the people who swing mops in the public buildings, dump bedpans in the County hospital, dig ditches, and perform other menial work. They don't work precincts regularly, although they help out at election time, but they do have to vote themselves and make sure their families vote, buy the usual tickets to political dinners, and in many wards, contribute about two per cent of their salaries to the ward organization.

Above the precinct captain is that lordly figure the ward committeeman, known in local parlance as "the clout," "the Chinaman," "the guy," and "our beloved leader."

Vito Marzullo is a ward committeeman and an alderman. He was born in Italy and has an elementary school education, but for years when he arrived at political functions, a judge walked a few steps behind him, moving ahead when there was a door to be opened. Marzullo had put him on the bench. His ward, on the near Southwest Side, is a pleasant stew of working class Italians, Poles, Mexicans, and blacks. A short, erect, tough, and likable man, he has had a Republican opponent only once in four elections to the City Council. Marzullo has about four hundred patronage jobs given to him by the Democratic Central Committee to fill. He has more jobs than some ward bosses because he has a stronger ward, with an average turnout of something like 14,500 Democrats to 1,200 Republicans. But he has fewer jobs than some other wards that are even stronger. Marzullo can tick off the jobs he fills:

From the book, *Boss: Richard J. Daley of Chicago* by Mike Royko. Copyright, 1971, by Mike Royko. Published by E. P. Dutton and Co. and used with their permission.

"I got an assistant state's attorney, and I got an assistant attorney general, I got an electrical inspector at twelve thousand dollars a year, and I got street inspectors and surveyors, and a county highway inspector. I got an administrative assistant to the zoning board and some people in the secretary of state's office. I got fifty-nine precinct captains and they all got assistants, and they all got good jobs. The lawyers I got in jobs don't have to work precincts, but they have to come to my ward office and give free legal advice to the people in the ward."

Service and favors, the staples of the precinct captain and his ward boss. The service may be nothing more than the ordinary municipal functions the citizen is paying taxes for. But there is always the feeling that they could slip if the precinct captain wants them to, that the garbage pickup might not be as good, that the dead tree might not be cut down.

Service and favors. In earlier days, the captain could do much more. The immigrant family looked to him as more than a link with a new and strange government: he was the government. He could tell them how to fill out their papers, how to pay their taxes, how to get a license. He was the welfare agency, with a basket of food and some coal when things got tough, and entree to the crowded charity hospital. He could take care of it when one of the kids got in trouble with the police. Social welfare agencies and better times took away many of his functions, but later there were still the traffic tickets to fix, the real estate tax assessments he might lower. When a downtown office didn't provide service, he was a direct link to government, somebody to cut through the bureaucracy.

In poor parts of the city, he has the added role of a threat. Don't vote, and you might lose your public housing apartment. Don't vote, and you might be cut off welfare. Don't vote, and you might have building inspectors poking around the house.

In the affluent areas, he is, sometimes, merely an errand boy, dropping off a tax bill on the way downtown, buying a vehicle sticker at City Hall, making sure that the streets are cleaned regularly, sounding out public opinion.

The payoff is on election day, when the votes are counted. If he produced, he is safe until the next election. If he didn't, that's it. "He has to go," Marzullo says. "If a company has a man who can't deliver, who can't sell the product, wouldn't he put somebody else in who can?"

Nobody except Chairman Daley knows precisely how many jobs the Machine controls. Some patronage jobs require special skills, so the jobholder doesn't have to do political work. Some are under civil service. And when the Republicans occasionally win a county office, the jobs change hands. There were more patronage jobs under the old Kelly-Nash Machine of the thirties and forties, but civil service reform efforts hurt the Machine. Some of the damage has been undone by Daley, however, who let civil service jobs slip back into patronage by giving tests infrequently or making them so difficult that few can pass, thus making it necessary to hire "temporary" employees, who stay "temporary" for the rest of their lives. Even civil service employees are subject to political pressures in the form of unwanted transfers, withheld promotions.

On certain special occasions, it is possible to see much of the Machine's patronage army assembled and marching. The annual St. Patrick's Day parade down State Street, with Daley leading the way, is a display of might that knots the stomachs of Republicans. An even more remarkable display of patronage power is seen at the State Fair, when on "Democrat Day" thousands of city workers are loaded into buses, trains, and cars which converge on the fairgrounds outside Springfield. The highlight of the fair is when Daley proudly hoofs down the middle of the grounds' dusty racetrack in ninety-degree heat with thousands of his sweating but devoted workers tramping behind him, wearing old-fashioned straw hats and derbies. The Illinois attorney general's staff of lawyers once thrilled the rustics with a crack manual of arms performance, using Daley placards instead of rifles.

Another reason the size of the patronage army is impossible

to measure is that it extends beyond the twenty to twenty-five thousand government jobs. The Machine has jobs at racetracks, public utilities, private industry, and the Chicago Transit Authority, which is the bus and subway system, and will help arrange easy union cards.

Out of the ranks of the patronage workers rise the Marzullos, fifty ward committeemen who, with thirty suburban township committeemen, sit as the Central Committee. For them the reward is more than a comfortable payroll job. If they don't prosper, it is because they are ignoring the advice of their Tammany cousin George Washington Plunkitt, who said, "I seen my opportunities and I took 'em." Chicago's ward bosses take 'em, too.

Most of them hold an elective office. Many of the Daley aldermen are ward bosses. Several are county commissioners. Others hold office as county clerk, assessor, or recorder of deeds and a few are congressmen and state legislators. Those who don't hold office are given top jobs running city departments, whether they know anything about the work or not. A ward boss who was given a $28,000-a-year job as head of the city's huge sewer system was asked what his experience was. "About twenty years ago I was a house drain inspector." "Did you ever work in the sewers?" "No, but many a time I lifted a lid to see if they were flowing." "Do you have an engineering background?" "Sort of. I took some independent courses at a school I forget the name of, and in 1932 I was a plumber's helper." His background was adequate: his ward usually carries by fifteen thousand to three thousand votes.

The elective offices and jobs provide the status, identity, and retinue of coat holders and door openers, but financially only the household money. About a third of them are lawyers, and the clients leap at them. Most of the judges came up through the Machine; many are former ward bosses themselves. This doesn't mean cases are always rigged, but one cannot underestimate the power of sentimentality. The political lawyers are greatly in demand for zoning disputes, big real estate ventures, and anything else that brings a company into contact with city agencies. When a New York corporation decided to bid for a lucrative Chicago cable TV franchise, they promptly tried to retain the former head of the city's legal department to represent them.

Those who don't have the advantage of a law degree turn to the old reliable, insurance. To be a success in the insurance field, a ward boss needs only two things: an office with his name on it and somebody in the office who knows how to write policies. All stores and businesses need insurance. Why not force the premium on the friendly ward boss? As Marzullo says, everybody needs favors.

One of the most successful political insurance firms is operated by party ancient Joe Gill. Gill gets a big slice of the city's insurance on public properties, like the Civic Center and O'Hare Airport. There are no negotiations or competitive bidding. The policies are given to him because he is Joe Gill. How many votes does Prudential Life deliver? The city's premiums are about $500,000 a year, giving Gill's firm a yearly profit of as much as $100,000.

Another firm, founded by the late Al Horan, and later operated by his heirs and County Assessor P. J. Cullerton, gets $100,000 a year in premiums from the city's park district. Since Cullerton is the man who sets the taxable value of all property in Cook County, it is likely that some big property owners would feel more secure being protected by his insurance.

When the city's sprawling lake front convention hall was built, the insurance business was tossed at the insurance firm founded by George Dunne, a ward boss and County Board president.

Another old-line firm is operated by John D'Arco, the crime syndicate's man in the Central Committee. He represents the First Ward, which includes the Loop, a goldmine of insurable property. D'Arco has never bothered to deny that he is a political appendage of the Mafia, probably because he knows that nobody would believe him. A denial would sound strained in light of his bad habit of being seen with Mafia bosses in public. Besides, the First Ward was controlled by the Mafia long before D'Arco became alderman and ward committeeman.

D'Arco's presence in the Central Committee has sometimes been an embarrassment to Chairman Daley. Despite D'Arco's understandable efforts to be discreet, he can't avoid personal publicity because the FBI is always following the people with whom he associates. When D'Arco announced that he was leaving the City Council because of poor health, while remaining ward committeeman, the FBI leaked the fact that Mafia chief Sam Giancana had ordered him out of the council in a pique over something or other. Giancana could do that, because it is his ward; D'Arco only watches it for him. One of Giancana's relatives has turned up as aide to a First Ward congressman. Another Giancana relative was elected to the state Senate. At Daley's urging, the First Ward organization made an effort to improve its image by running a young banker for alderman. But the banker finally resigned from the council, saying that being the First Ward's alderman was ruining his reputation.

When he is asked about the First Ward, Daley retreats to the democratic position that the people elect D'Arco and their other representatives, and who is he to argue with the people? He has the authority, as party chairman, to strip the First Ward, or any ward, of its patronage, and there are times when he surely must want to do so. Raids on Syndicate gambling houses sometimes turn up city workers, usually sponsored by the First Ward organization. While he has the authority to take away the jobs, it would cause delight in the press and put him in the position of confirming the Mafia's participation in the Machine. He prefers to suffer quietly through the periodic flaps.

The question is often raised whether he actually has the power, in addition to the authority, to politically disable the Mafia. It has been in city government longer than he has, and has graduated its political lackeys to judgeships, the various legislative bodies, and positions throughout government. While it no longer is the controlling force it was in Thompson's administration, or as arrogantly obvious as it was under Kelly-Nash, it remains a part of the Machine, and so long as it doesn't challenge him but is satisfied with its limited share, Daley can live with it, just as he lives with the rascals in Springfield.

Ward bosses are men of ambition, so when they aren't busy with politics or their outside professions, they are on the alert for "deals." At any given moment, a group of them, and their followers, are either planning a deal, hatching a deal, or looking for a deal.

Assessor Cullerton and a circle of his friends have gone in for buying up stretches of exurban land for golf courses, resorts, and the like. Others hold interests in racetracks, which depend on political goodwill for additional racing dates.

The city's dramatic physical redevelopment has been a boon to the political worlds as well as the private investors. There are so many deals involving ranking members of the Machine that it has been suggested that the city slogan be changed from *Urbs In Horto*, which means "City in a Garden," to *Ubi Est Mea*, which means "Where's mine?"

From where Daley sits, alone atop the Machine, he sees all the parts, and his job is to keep them functioning properly. One part that has been brought into perfect synchronization is organized labor — perhaps the single biggest factor in the unique survival of the big city organization in Chicago. Labor provides Daley with his strongest personal support and contributes great sums to his campaigns. Daley's roots are deep in organized labor. His father was an organizer of his sheet-metal workers' local, and Bridgeport was always a union neighborhood. With politics and the priesthood, union activity was one of the more heavily traveled roads to success. Daley grew up with Steve Bailey, who became head of the Plumbers' Union, and as Daley developed politically, Bailey brought him into contact with other labor leaders.

Thousands of trade union men are employed by local government. Unlike the federal government and many other cities, Chicago always pays the top construction rate, rather than the lower maintenance scale, although most of the work is maintenance. Daley's massive public works projects, gilded with overtime pay in his rush to cut ribbons before elections, are another major source of union jobs.

His policy is that a labor leader be appointed to every policy-making city board or committee. In recent years, it has worked out this way: the head of the Janitors' Union was on the police board, the park board, the Public Buildings Commission, and several others. The head of the Plumbers' Union was on the Board of Health and ran the St. Patrick's Day parade. The head of the Electricians' Union was vice-president of the Board of Education. The Clothing Workers' Union had a man on the library board. The Municipal Employees' Union boss was on the Chicago Housing Authority, which runs the city's public housing projects. The head of the Chicago Federation of Labor and somebody from the Teamsters' Union were helping run the poverty program. And the sons of union officials find the door to City Hall open if they decide on a career in politics.

The third major part of the Machine is money. Once again, only Daley knows how much it has and how it is spent. As party chairman, he controls its treasury. The spending is lavish. Even when running against a listless nobody, Daley may spend a million dollars. The amount used for "precinct money," which is handed out to the precinct captains and used in any way that helps bring out the Democratic vote, can exceed the entire Republican campaign outlay. This can mean paying out a couple of dollars or a couple of chickens to voters in poor neighborhoods, or bottles of cheap wine in the Skid Row areas. Republicans claim that the Democrats will spend as much as $300,000 in precinct money alone for a city election. To retain a crucial office, such as that of county assessor, hundreds of thousands have been spent on billboard advertising alone. Add to that the TV and radio saturation, and the spending for local campaigning exceeds by far the cost-per-vote level of national campaigning.

The money comes from countless sources. From the patronage army, it goes into the ward offices as dues, and part of it is turned over to party headquarters. Every ward leader throws his annual $25-a-head golf days, corned beef dinners, and picnics. The ticket books are thrust at the patronage workers and they either sell them or, as they say, "eat them," bearing the cost themselves.

There are "ward books," with page after page of advertising, sold by precinct workers to local businesses and other favorseekers, Alderman Marzullo puts out a 350-page ad book every year, at one hundred dollars a page. There are no blank pages in his book. The ward organizations keep what they need to function, and the rest is funneled to party headquarters.

Contractors may be the biggest of all contributors. Daley's public works program has poured billions into their pockets, and they in turn have given millions back to the party in contributions. Much of it comes from contractors who are favored, despite the seemingly fair system of competitive bidding. In some fields, only a handful of contractors ever bid, and they manage to arrange things so that at the end of the year each has received about the same amount of work and the same profit. A contractor who is not part of this "brotherhood" refrains from bidding on governmental work. If he tries to push his way in by submitting a reasonable bid, which would assure him of being the successful low bidder, he may suddenly find that the unions are unable to supply him with the workers he needs.

Even Republican businessmen contribute money to the Machine, more than they give to Republican candidates. Republicans can't do anything for them, but Daley can. . . .

The Future of Machine Politics

From its inception, citizens charged the political machine with waste, corruption, inefficiency, and immorality. Reformers periodically attacked the machine from every angle, yet the machine continued to exist despite the attacks. Since World War II, however, many cities have abandoned boss politics. Will boss politics completely disappear in the last half of the twentieth century?

In this reading, Edward Banfield and James Wilson, experts on municipal government, discuss the future of political machine. Arguing that fundamental changes in the nature of urban life have occurred, the authors contend that the political machine is now obsolete. Earlier political machines fulfilled needs that, according to Banfield and Wilson, no longer exist or can be more easily satisfied by other governmental agencies. They argue, moreover, that the increasingly sophisticated voting public refuses to vote along strict party lines. Old needs and old loyalties no longer exist. Do you agrew with the authors' thesis that machine politics is obsolete? What type of government will replace the political machine?

The main reason for the decline and near disappearance of the city-wide machine was — and is — the growing unwillingness of voters to accept the inducements that it offered. The petty favors and "friendship" of the precinct captains declined in value as immigrants were assimilated, public welfare programs were vastly extended, and *per capita* incomes rose steadily and sharply in war and postwar prosperity. To the voter who in case of need could turn to a professional social worker and receive as a matter of course unemployment compensation, aid to dependent children, old-age assistance, and all the rest, the precinct captain's hod of coal was a joke.

Only those who are least competent to cope with the conditions of modern life, those who are culturally or personally incapacitated in one way or another, still value and seek the "favors" of the machine. They are, of course, the poorest of the poor, especially Negro slum dwellers, rooming-house drifters, criminals, and near criminals. Nowadays there is little that the machine can do for such people except to give them information about where to go and whom to see in the city bureaucracy and (what is probably more important, despite its illusory character) to give them the feeling that they have a friend and protector. The ward leader cannot arrange to have welfare payments made to someone not entitled to them; he can, however, tell a needy person who *is* entitled to payments how to apply for them. In doing so, he may, of course, manage to leave the impression that if he had not made a telephone call and used his "influence" as a "friend" the payments would never have been made. Even his opportunities to serve the voter by giving information (and thus to lay the basis for a later claim upon him) diminish, however, as the giving of information and other functions which are the politicians' special stock in trade are transferred to the executive departments. As Mayor Clark of Philadelphia remarked, "When the word gets around that you can't get things done by favor anymore, there tends to be a sort of channeling of complaints and desires to get things done away from the legislative branch and into the executive branch."

"Friendship" is also harder to give. One reason is television. The precinct captain who visits in the evening interrupts a television program and must either stay and watch in silence or else excuse himself quickly and move on. Another reason is the changing ethnic character of the inner city. When, for example, a white neighborhood is "invaded" by Negroes, the white precinct captain cannot, or will not, form friendships among them as easily as he does among whites. He may even be afraid to enter a tenement of Negroes after dark. In time he will be replaced by a Negro captain, but meanwhile the organization suffers.

While the value to the voter of what the machine offers has declined, the value to him of what he has to give — his vote — has increased. This has happened because of the changing class character of the electorate. Except in the inner parts of the larger central cities, the proportion of middle-class people is greater than it was. Machine-style politics has rarely worked in predominantly middle-class districts. People who have, or pretend to have, opinions on political questions will not give away their votes or exchange them for petty favors. Middle-class people do not want the precinct captain's "friendship" or the ward leader's help. It is easy for them to be virtuous in these matters: they don't have to worry about getting into the county hospital or out of the county jail. And they generally resent his efforts at persuasion. They think of themselves as well informed, able to make up their own minds, independent. Being qualified to pass upon public questions follows from their education status, they think, and therefore exhibiting the qualifications is a matter of pride. Whether justified or not, these claims to political competence make it hard for the precinct captain to exercise influence. Recently a Chicago captain told of calling on a voter one Sunday afternoon and finding him with three newspapers spread out on the floor and the TV set on. "What can you tell me that I don't already know?" the voter asked.

The assimilation of lower-class people into the middle class has, of course, entailed their assimilation to the political ethos of the Anglo-Saxon-Protestant elite, the central idea of which is that politics should be based on public rather than on private motives and, accordingly, should stress the virtues of honesty, impartiality, and efficiency.

Wherever the middle class is dominant, this ethos prevails and fixes the character of the political system. If, as seems likely, the middle class will in the very long run assimilate the lower class entirely, the final extinction of the machine is probably guaranteed.

Meanwhile, there remain enclaves that are heavily lower-class in all of the central cities and many of the older suburbs. In these, machine-style politics is as popular as ever. It does not flourish as of old, however, because of restraints and impediments imposed by the middle class, which constitutes the majority in the metropolitan area if not in the city proper, controls the legislatures, and has a virtual monopoly on federal office, both elective and appointive.

Some machines, however, are managing to adjust to the changing circumstances and to substitute, little by little as necessary, one kind of inducement for another so that they gradually become less machine-like. The Chicago machine is one which has survived by "reforming" itself piecemeal. The dynamics of its adaption are worth examining briefly.

The central city of Chicago is overwhelmingly Democratic, but the outlying wards are moderately or strongly Republican. If the "country towns" (actually suburbs which lie in Cook County) are included, Cook County is marginally but not "solidly" Democratic. If a boss were concerned only with the central city, the old style of machine politics would work well enough. In fact, however, he must try to carry the county and the state for the party. Their loss would deprive him of patronage, expose him to hostile acts by a Republican state's attorney, sheriff, governor, and state legislature, and weaken his power in the councils of the party. He must therefore appeal as well as he can to the independent and Republican voters who live in the outlying wards and suburbs. To do this, he must minimize, or at least render inconspicuous, his use of patronage and payoffs, and he must exert himself to find "blue ribbon" candidates for important offices and "professional" administrators for important departments and to inaugurate civic projects that will suit the "good government" voter without costing very much. In effect, he must take political resources away from those central-city wards where the machine is strong and give them to the independent voters in the "newspaper" wards and in the independent suburbs, thereby, of course, creating disaffection among his machine lieutenants. Every step taken in the direction of appeasing the independent voter is, of course, a step towards destruction of the machine.

The civic projects that Mayor Daley inaugurated in Chicago — street cleaning, street lighting, road building, a new airport, and a convention hall for example — were shrewdly chosen. They were highly visible; they benefited the county as well as the city; for the most part they were noncontroversial; they did not require much increase in taxes; and they created many moderately paying jobs that politicians could dispense as patronage. The Mayor's program conspicuously neglected the goals of militant Negroes, demands for the enforcement of the building code, and (until there was a dramatic exposé) complaints about police inefficiency and corruption. These things were all controversial, and, perhaps most important, would have no immediate, visible result; either they would benefit those central-city voters whose loyalty could be counted upon anyway or else (as in the case of police reform) they threatened to hurt the machine in a vital spot.

Other big-city machines have not adapted as successfully. The Pendergast machine in Kansas City was destroyed. Carmine DeSapio's efforts to refurbish the "image" of Tammany Hall in Manhattan not only failed but actually seemed to incite reformers to attack more energetically. Why is it that most machines did not adapt and survive as the Chicago machine has?

One reason is that the bosses have been too greedy for money. Tom Pendergast, for example, gambled heavily at the race tracks and thereby placed himself in a position where, even if he wanted to, he could not afford to cut the "take." Daley, by contrast, has not enriched himself. The satisfactions he gets from politics are apparently of an entirely different sort, and this has enabled him to use greedy lieutenants without exciting their envy and to gain personally in prestige, power, and whatever other such values he seeks by making reforms.

Some machines failed to adapt because their leaders waited too long before making reforms. The leader who makes a reform only under duress is not likely to be able to salvage the situation by making it on his own terms. This is what happened in New York. Carmine DeSapio tried in the early 1950's to remodel Tammany Hall but the power of the machine had by then withered away to such an extent that he could not make the kinds of changes in the situation that would have saved the organization.

In a word, the machines failed because bosses lacked statesmanship. Colonel Jacob Arvey, who persuaded Mayor Kelly to step down and the ward leaders to endure the eight-year Kennelly drought of reform, and Mayor Daley, who then took the initiative in reform, are exceptions to the general rule. The "accident" of their presence in Chicago probably accounts more than anything else for the strength of the party there. James Finnegan, who brought Philadelphia's regular Democratic organization into temporary alliance with the "blue blood" reformers, Joseph S. Clark and Richardson Dilworth, seems to have been another such statesman. In Philadelphia, as in Chicago, the machine suffered temporarily by reform. By 1960, however, the reformers were fast fading from the scene.

It goes without saying that a system of government based upon specific, material inducements is wholly at odds with that conception of democracy which says that decisions ought to be made on the basis of reasonable discussion about what the common good requires. Machine government is, essentially, a system of organized bribery.

The destruction of machines would therefore be good if it did no more than to permit government on the basis of appropriate motives, that is, public-regarding ones. In fact, it has other highly desirable consequences — especially greater honesty, impartiality and (in routine matters) efficiency. This last gain deserves special emphasis because it is one that the machine (or its boss) cannot, in the nature of the case, adopt at its own initiative. A boss, who, like Mayor Daley of Chicago, has with great effort centralized, to an extreme degree, political influence cannot be expected to turn around and delegate to subordinates that influence so that city government can be carried on expeditiously and without obtaining the mayor's (i.e., the boss's) approval on all matters, however, trivial.

Great as the advantages of reform are, they are at least partly offset by certain disadvantages. Because these disadvantages are less obvious than the advantages, we will focus our attention upon them. In doing so we do not, of course, imply any derogation of the values sought by reformers.

The machine served certain latent social functions, functions which no one intended but which presumably would have had to be served by another means if not by that one. This has been remarked by Robert Merton, David Riesman, and other sociologists. According to Merton, it humanized and personalized assistance to the needy; afforded businesses, including illicit ones, privileges that they needed in order to survive; provided a route of social mobility for persons to whom other routes were closed; and was an antidote to the constitutional dispersal of authority.

The last item on this list is of particular interest here. As we showed in the last chapter, the decentralization of authority in the city must be overcome in one way or another if public undertakings are to be carried forward. A system of specific, material inducements (i.e., a machine) is not, we explained, the only way of bringing about a centralization of influence; in principle, measures to weaken the machine may be accompanied by other measures to centralize influence. In fact, however, this never seems to happen; if any substitute at all is provided for the power of the boss, it is a partial one. La Guardia's reforms in New York, Clark and Dilworth's in Philadelphia, and Daley's in Chicago, although strengthening administrative authority, nevertheless weakened the influence of the city government as a whole. Because of this weakening of the city government, the reform of the machine, although increasing efficiency in routine matters, may at the same time have decreased it in those more important matters which call for the exercise of political power.

The Chicago police scandals of 1960 are a case in point. Mayor Daley's excessive regard for the opinion of the "good government" forces restrained him from taking measures which might have prevented these scandals. He had inherited a civil service system which in effect put control of the police department in the hands of its senior officers (neither he nor the commissioner could fire a policeman), and — again to avoid the charge of "playing politics" — he did not ask the legislature for authority to reorganize the department.

The machine provided the politician with a base of influence deriving from its control of lower-income voters. As this base shrinks, he becomes more dependent on other sources of influence — especially newspapers, civic associations, labor unions, business groups, and churches. "Nonpolitical" (really nonparty) lines of access to the city administration are substituted for "political" ones. Campaign funds come not from salary kickbacks and the sale of favors, but from rich men and from companies doing business with the city. Department heads and other administrators who are able to command the support of professional associations and civic groups become indispensable to the mayor and are therefore harder for him to control. Whereas the spoils of office formerly went to "the boys" in the delivery wards in the form of jobs and favors, they now go in the form of urban renewal projects, street cleaning, and better police protection to newspaper wards. Better police protection in white neighborhoods means greater police harassment in Negro ones. Appointment of white experts means non-appointment of Negro politicians.

Even though in the abstract one may prefer a government that gets its influence from reasonable discussion about the common good rather than from giving jobs, favors, and "friendship," even though in the abstract he may prefer government by middle-class to government by lower-class standards, and even though in the abstract he may prefer the rule of professional administrators to that of politicians, he may nevertheless favor the machine in some particular concrete situation. The choice is never between the machine and some ideal alternative. If there is any choice at all — and in some instances there may not be — it is between it and some real — and therefore imperfect — alternative. It is at least conceivable that in some of the large central cities the political indifferentism of the machine may be preferable to any likely alternative.

Suggestions for Further Reading

The extensive list of historical literature dealing with nineteenth- and twentieth-century boss politics has grown dramatically during the last quarter century. New approaches and interpretations provide a greater understanding of the complex issues and functions surrounding the phenomenon of the urban boss. This selective bibliography provides a brief introduction to the major works which focus on boss politics.

The theoretical literature on the rise of the city boss and the urban political machine is substantial. It should be examined by anyone desiring an understanding of the development of the boss system. The best of the theoretical works include: Edward Banfield and James Q. Wilson, *City Politics* (New York, 1968); Robert A. Dahl, *Who Governs? Democracy and Power in an American City* (New Haven, 1969); Harold Gosnell, *Machine Politics: Chicago Model* (Chicago, 1937); Fred Greenstein, *The American Party System and the American People* (New Jersey, 1970) and Robert K. Merton, *Social Theory and Social Structure* (New York, 1968). A recent attempt to generalize from the careers of several bosses over the last 100 years is John M. Allswang, *Bosses, Machines, and*

Urban Voters (Port Washington, New York, 1977). A basic survey of several bosses plus a sampling of the analytical literature is Alexander Callow's *The City Boss in America* (New York, 1976). Finally readers should not neglect the now dated yet still important book by Harold Zink, *City Bosses in the United States* (Durham, North Carolina, 1939).

The colorful, if often unscrupulous, nineteenth century bosses examined in part I have been the subjects of numerous full length studies. Works on New York City's bosses include Seymour Mandelbaum, *Boss Tweed's New York* (New York, 1965); Alexander B. Callow, Jr., *The Tweed Ring* (New York, 1966); and Jerome Mushkat, *Tammany: The Evolution of a Political Machine, 1789-1865* (Syracuse, 1971). Recently Leo Hershkowitz, *Tweed's New York: Another Look* (Garden City, New York, 1977) has contested the generally unfavorable view of Tweed.

For contemporary accounts of nineteenth-century machine politics, readers should consult: James Bryce, *The American Commonwealth* (New York, 1893); M. Ostrogorski, *Democracy and the Organization of Political Parties*, translated from the French by Frederick Clark (Vol. II, New York, 1964); Lincoln Steffens, *The Shame of the Cities* (New York, 1957) and William L. Riordan, *Plunkitt of Tammany Halls*, (New York, 1948).

During the last decade a number of important studies have examined the concept of the boss-reformer. Using specific urban political systems as case studies, many historians suggest that the reform-minded mayor often had to use machine tactics to achieve his goals. Others argue that bosses often posed as reformers. Studies of reform bosses in urban America include: Melvin G. Holli, *Reform in Detroit: Hazen S. Pingree and Urban Politics* (New York, 1969); Gerald Kurland, *Seth Low: The Reformer in an Urban-Industrial Age* (New York, 1971); Edwin R. Lewinson, *John Purroy Mitchell: The Boy Mayor of New York* (New York, 1965). Other important reform bosses are examined in Arthur Mann, *LaGuardia Comes to Power* (Philadelphia, 1965); Zane Miller, *Boss Cox's*

Cincinnati: Urban Politics in the Progressive Era (New York, 1968) and Jack Tager, *The Intellectual as Urban Reformer: Brand Whitlock and the Progressive Movement* (Forest Grove, Oregon, 1968). Useful selections of the literature on bosses and reformers are Blaine Brownell and Warren Stickel, *Bosses and Reformers* (Boston, 1973) and Bruce Stave, *Urban Bosses, Machines, and Progressive Reformers* (Boston, 1972).

For an in-depth account of Cleveland's boss-reformer during the Progressive Era, readers may wish to consult the following contemporary accounts: Tom L. Johnson, *My Story* (New York, 1911); Carl Lorenz, *Tom L. Johnson* (New York, 1911) and Frederic Howe, *Confessions of a Reformer* (New York, 1925).

A number of excellent studies of twentieth-century political bosses in specific cities are available. Chicago and New York, of course, have been studied most frequently. In addition to works previously cited, full length studies on Chicago include: Joel A. Tarr, *A Study of Boss Politics: William Lorimer of Chicago* (Urbana, Illinois, 1971); Alex Gottfried, *Boss Cermak of Chicago* (Seattle, 1962); William F. Gleason, *Daley of Chicago: The Man, The Mayor and the Limits of Conventional Politics* (New York 1970); Len O'Connor, *Clout: Mayor Daley and His City* (New York, 1975); and Mike Royko, *Boss: Richard J. Daley of Chicago* (New York, 1971). Peter Yessne's, *Quotations from Mayor Daley* (New York, 1969) is a modern-day version of Riordan's *Plunkitt of Tammany Hall.*

For other New York political bosses see, Nancy Weiss, *Charles Francis Murphey, 1958-1924: Respectability and Responsibility in Tammany Politics* (Northampton, Massachusetts, 1968) and Theodore Lowi, *At the Pleasure of the Mayor: Patronage and Power in New York City, 1898-1954* (New York, 1964).

Important studies on other twentieth century bosses include: Walton E. Bean, *Boss Ruef's San Francisco* (Berkeley, 1952); James B. Crooks, *Politics and Progress: The Rise of Urban Progressivism in Baltimore, 1895-1911* (New York,

1968); Lyle W. Dorsett, *The Pendergast Machine* (New York, 1968); William D. Miller, *Memphis During the Progressive Era, 1900-1917* (Providence, Rhode Island, 1957); Bruce M. Stave, *The New Deal and the Last Hurrah: Pittsburgh Machine Politics* (Pittsburgh, 1970); Lyle Dorsett, *Franklin D. Roosevelt and the City Bosses* (Port Washington, New York, 1977).